For Parents

What Makes
Your
Teenager
Tick

By Dr. G. Keith Olson

**Family
Tree™
Group**

Loveland, Colorado

Dedication

*To all parents who are engaged in the
difficult task of lovingly guiding their
teenage children while letting them
go at the same time.*

Acknowledgments

This book wouldn't exist without the commitment and skillful work of my friend and editor, Cindy Hansen. Her scalpel and suture are the pen and cursor. She wields them with sensitivity, keen perception and determination to create a product that will minister to the reader in a pleasurable rather than arduous package. For this, Cindy, I thank you.

I want to express my gratitude to Dawn Goto for her meticulous copy editing and offer thank yous to Nancy Shaw and Sharon Mattson for their valuable part in the manuscript's preparation.

What Makes *Your* Teenager Tick
Copyright © 1988 by G. Keith Olson
First Printing

Credits
Edited by Cindy Hansen
Designed by Judy Atwood

Scripture quotations are from the Holy Bible, New International Version. Copyright © 1973, 1978, 1984 International Bible Society. Used by permission of Zondervan Bible Publishers.
ISBN 0931-529-75-1
Printed in the United States of America

Contents

Introduction **5**

Chapter 1 *The Power-Oriented Personality* **9**
Development of the Power-Oriented Personality 9
Healthy Forms of the Power-Oriented Personality 11
Unhealthy Forms of the Power-Oriented Personality 15
Effects of Power-Oriented Behavior on Others 18
Guidelines for Parenting Power-Oriented Adolescents 19

Chapter 2 *The Competitive Personality* **29**
Development of the Competitive Personality 30
Healthy Forms of the Competitive Personality 32
Unhealthy Forms of the Competitive Personality 37
Effects of Competitive Behavior on Others 42
Guidelines for Parenting Competitive Adolescents 43

Chapter 3 *The Aggressive Personality* **55**
Development of the Aggressive Personality 56
Healthy Forms of the Aggressive Personality 59
Unhealthy Forms of the Aggressive Personality 63
Effects of Aggressive Behavior on Others 69
Guidelines for Parenting Aggressive Adolescents 71

Chapter 4 *The Rebellious Personality* **81**
Development of the Rebellious Personality 82
Healthy Forms of the Rebellious Personality 85
Unhealthy Forms of the Rebellious Personality 88
Effects of Rebellious Behavior on Others 92
Guidelines for Parenting Rebellious Adolescents 93

Chapter 5 *The Self-Demeaning Personality* **105**
Development of the Self-Demeaning Personality 106
Healthy Forms of the Self-Demeaning Personality 109
Unhealthy Forms of the Self-Demeaning Personality 113
Effects of Self-Demeaning Behavior on Others 120
Guidelines for Parenting Self-Demeaning Adolescents 120

Chapter 6 **The Dependent Personality** **133**
   Development of the Dependent Personality 134
   Healthy Forms of the Dependent Personality 137
   Unhealthy Forms of the Dependent Personality 143
   Effects of Dependent Behavior on Others 148
   Guidelines for Parenting Dependent Adolescents 150

Chapter 7 **The Conforming Personality** **161**
   Development of the Conforming Personality 162
   Healthy Forms of the Conforming Personality 167
   Unhealthy Forms of the Conforming Personality 171
   Effects of Conforming Behavior on Others 177
   Guidelines for Parenting Conforming Adolescents 178

Chapter 8 **The Responsible Personality** **189**
   Development of the Responsible Personality 190
   Healthy Forms of the Responsible Personality 195
   Unhealthy Forms of the Responsible Personality 199
   Effects of Responsible Behavior on Others 204
   Guidelines for Parenting Responsible Adolescents 205

Closing Comments **216**

Introduction

"My son, Dave, always compares himself with everybody else. He doesn't feel okay if another kid can do something better than he can. Why does he have to be the best?"

"I wish I could get Sondra involved with other kids. She's so shy! It's like she's afraid of rejection, so she won't let anyone get to know her. What made her that way?"

"My daughter Kerrie is just the opposite. She loves attention and always strives to be the leader of any group she's in. Why can't she just relax and enjoy being one of the kids?"

"Now you're talking about my son. Jeremy has to be like everyone else. He can't stand on his own two feet. How can I help him develop more inner strength?"

"I wish my second child, Bart, wasn't so cynical about everyone and everything. His critical remarks and putdowns are painful to those around him. How can I encourage him to have a more positive attitude?"

"I've got a real rebel on my hands. Sarah reacts angrily and defiantly to almost everything anybody asks her to do. How can we keep the family together while we help her through these difficult years?"

During a recent meeting parents of junior and senior high students discussed these situations. These concerned parents vented their feelings and frustrations about the children they love. But the meeting also provided valid answers to their questions and offered practical help for solving difficult parenting problems. And that's the goal for writing this book.

As a parent you'll discover eight basic social interaction styles:

Power-Oriented Personality

Competitive Personality

Aggressive Personality

Rebellious Personality

Self-Demeaning Personality

Dependent Personality

Conforming Personality

Responsible Personality

One of these styles will describe your teenager's typical way of handling interpersonal situations. But you'll also find aspects of your teenager in some other styles. By identifying your young person's preferred social orientation, you'll understand the needs, emotions, wishes and internal conflicts your child expresses. You'll also recognize both the healthy and unhealthy expression of each social orientation.

Each personality trait has both a positive and negative side. For example, compulsiveness can lead to increased productivity or paralysis. Whether the trait is healthy or unhealthy depends on answers to two questions:

• How extreme or intense is the teenager's behavior?

• How appropriate is the behavior in a specific situation?

Your teenager's behaviors are generally healthier if they're moderate and appropriate. But all young people move along a continuum between extremely healthy and extremely unhealthy behavior. As a parent you'll want to nudge your young person toward the healthy end of the continuum.

If you're concerned that your teenager may be locked in an unhealthy pattern, consider contacting a professional counselor or therapist. Ask your minister, youth minister, physician or school counselor. Check to see that the therapist is licensed to practice in your state. Make sure he or she specializes or has experience in working with teenagers. If possible find a Christian counselor who meets these qualifications.

What Makes Your *Teenager Tick* is a condensed version of *Why Teenagers Act the Way They Do*. It helps you as a parent better understand the confusing behavior you often see in your teenager. This book gives you specific and prac-

tical guidelines on how you can best respond to your teenager. You'll also discover:

• How to carefully and accurately observe your teenager's
behavior.

• How to identify your child's primary style of social interaction.

• What personal needs and fears your teenager is expressing through his or her behavior.

• How best to respond to your teenager to meet his or
her needs without making the situation worse.

As you read this book and, more importantly, as you observe your young person's behavior, recognize God's creative spirit at work. Avoid making "good" and "bad"
judgments too quickly. Every personality trait has positive
and negative characteristics. Your job (and mine) as a parent
is to help your teenager develop as fully as possible into the
person God created him or her to be. This book is dedicat-
ed to assist you in that wonderful and important mission.

CHAPTER ONE

The Power-Oriented Personality

Teenagers who develop a power-oriented personality often appear strong, confident and secure. Peers view them as "having it all together." Adults view them as surprisingly mature for their age. But upon closer evaluation, we find these adolescents have developed a defense system that merely gives the appearance of well-integrated strength.

Power-oriented teenagers are most comfortable when they feel strong and self-reliant. These young people are most concerned with dominance. They need to see themselves in control of their lives. They want the capacity to predict what will happen to them. Therefore, these young people don't welcome surprises. Even surprise birthday parties threaten power-oriented teenagers because of their loss of control. They must maintain control over other people and activities to feel comfortable in their environment.

Power-oriented adolescents are usually ambitious and goal-directed. They "make things happen" at church, home and school. Ambition propels them toward higher goals, and attaining those goals reinforces their feelings of personal worth and value. They closely associate their self-worth and importance with their performance and success.

► Development of the Power-Oriented Personality

The use of power is a natural part of identity formation,

adolescents' crucial developmental task. Making their own decisions contributes to young people's successful individuation (separation) from their parents. Without increasing self-control and making active choices in life, adolescents don't mature into independent adults. Several factors can influence development of the power-oriented personality type.

1. High energy output. Good physical health and stamina are essential for sustaining power-oriented teenagers. Without proper nutrition, adequate rest and sufficient exercise, these adolescents have difficulty maintaining their strong power-related defenses.

2. Reinforcement for using power to enhance their self-esteem. Some kids earn outstanding grades and academic honors in schedules filled with college preparatory courses. Others attain popular acclaim, peer respect and special privileges as payoffs for their election to student government or church youth group offices. Athletic achievements provide powerful respect and numerous honors to even more young people. Some adolescents' ambitious efforts in business may be reinforced by financial gain. The rewards for power are numerous and influential.

3. Powerful role models. Parents provide the most powerful role models. For example, fathers and mothers who value achievement in their own lives often produce children who adopt that value as well. Other authority figures (such as teachers, youth ministers, adult relatives and adult friends) also impact these teenagers. When these respected adults model power-oriented defense mechanisms, young people tend to imitate those same behaviors.

4. Psychological and physical pain and injury. Some young people have suffered from severe parenting throughout their childhood. Parents who struggle with alcohol, character disorders and abusive tendencies sometimes discipline their children so severely that they ensure psychological injury. Harsh physical discipline, parental neglect, excessive roughness and mean or vicious teasing can lead to the child's physical injury. Experience assures us that psychological damage always accompanies physical injury. For these children, the inability to control their environment has had brutally painful and damaging results. They've learned a hard lesson by placing themselves under another's care or control. For these teenagers, not to be strong and powerful means to be vulnerable to danger, even from people who say they love them.

Many teenagers have created painful situations for themselves by responding to an impulse during a lapse in self-control. While drunk or high on drugs, some have had car accidents or committed sexual or violent acts. Power-oriented adolescents develop their defense system as a direct result of experiencing pain, discomfort or injury during times they weren't in control. These teenagers believe control of themselves and their environment is essential for their security.

5. Parents who exercise excessive control. Some overprotective parents block every effort their children make to grow up. As a result, they discourage their children and teach them self-doubt. Deep feelings of guilt, burning resentment and intense anger result from these types of childhood experiences. These young people have to develop great resources of internal strength and courage to break these restrictive bonds and succeed in life.

Certainly, there are more variables that can contribute to the development of a power-oriented personality. However, most of these teenagers have been strongly influenced by one or more of these five contributing factors.

► Healthy Forms of the Power-Oriented Personality

Teenagers who develop a controlled, balanced use of power usually succeed quite well as adolescents. Our society values and reinforces use of strength. Those who handle power in positive, constructive ways receive great esteem from others. Adolescents may find several positive expressions for their power-oriented defense systems.

The following examples represent two patterns of the healthy power-oriented personality type; however, both examples are extreme. "Leaders" such as Phillip seek personal comfort by controlling both themselves and others. "Brains" such as Stephanie avoid anxiety by focusing on their own ambition and ability while avoiding the less predictable world of social interaction. As long as these patterns remain moderate and under control, they can be quite healthy.

The Leader. Leadership positions provide natural, constructive outlets for this power-oriented adolescent. Phillip is a good example of this leadership pattern. The oldest of four children, Phillip grew up in a loving, moderately strict home. His parents insisted on responsibility, honesty and adherence to other traditional values. Each child was responsible for regularly completing chores. School grades were important, though academic excellence wasn't stressed. The parents often told their children, "We just expect you to do your best." Not knowing exactly what his best was, Phillip grew up with the idea he probably could (and should) do better in most everything he tried.

As most oldest children do, Phillip tried eagerly to please his parents. Since traditional values were important in his household, he accepted them as his own. Phillip ordered his life around responsibility, integrity and strength. He absorbed and expressed the Christian values of helpfulness, generosity and care for others. He felt much better about himself when he was strong, useful and in control.

During junior high Phillip began running for student body offices. He won most of his elections from that time through his senior year. Although campaigning for office made him uncomfortable, he enjoyed fulfilling the job's requirements when he'd won.

Phillip's church youth group provided another place for him to utilize his leadership gifts. He attended a small church where only a few people possessed real leadership qualities. Recognizing his gifts, the adults always chose Phillip when they needed youth group representation on committees.

By Phillip's junior year, he realized he felt best about himself when he was operating in some leadership capacity. He felt more confident when he was in control. Phillip recognized his discomfort around new people his own age, but he also felt uneasy in any unstructured group of his friends. With no leadership role to dictate his behavior, he didn't know how to act or what to say. He withdrew from close friendships and usually declined party invitations unless he had some prescribed role to fill.

Phillip depended more and more on a leadership position for self-esteem. Since his effectiveness in that role brought sufficient praise and respect, he seldom consciously experienced any insecurity or self-doubt. For only brief moments did Phillip actually question whether people liked him for who he was. At these times of sensitivity he felt most people valued him only for what he could do for them. In response to those painful instances of loneliness and alienation, he quickly re-entered his leadership pattern where he regained self-value.

The Brain. Some power-oriented teenagers aren't as concerned with leadership power. These young people just want to feel safe within themselves. If they control their world adequately, they feel secure. That sense of security usually requires these power-oriented adolescents to maintain emotional distance from their peers. Stephanie is a good example of this expression of the power-oriented personality: the "brain."

Stephanie is the second of four children. She has an older brother who excels in athletics, a real star on the playing field. Her younger brother and sister are in elementary school. The younger children are average academic students active in activities normal for that age.

School has always been easy for Stephanie. She learned to read and write earlier than most children. Although she works hard at her studies, she believes in her natural ability to consistently earn straight "A's." Teachers continuously praise her classroom behavior, making "Stephanie" and "teacher's pet" synonymous terms in her peer group.

As she progressed through junior high, Stephanie relied increasingly on her intelligence as the basis for her self-concept. Her self-esteem during high school depended almost entirely on her continuing ability to perform academically. However, because she concentrated so hard on only one area of her life, problems appeared during her sophomore year. She began avoiding friends, parties and other social gatherings.

"I'd like to go skating with you, but I've got to study for my chemistry exam tonight."

"Jill's birthday party sounds like a lot of fun, but I'm a little behind in algebra."

Stephanie withdrew more and more from her friends. Her studies replaced her social life. Now a high school sophomore, she feels too socially insecure to accept invitations, and she's invited less often.

Stephanie created her own sphere of comfort. Greatly reinforced for her academic performance as a child, she made that the focus of her identity. But she went too far. By concentrating her energies on academics, she withdrew from the uncertainties of the interpersonal world of relationships.

Stephanie felt competent and in control of her academic world. She knew what to expect. She could predict the outcome and had some control of her future as long as she focused on academics. If she studied diligently, she got "A's." It was that simple.

But Stephanie didn't have that kind of control in her social environment. When she entered her social world, she was unsure of herself and others. She couldn't accurately predict what would happen and felt she had little control of her future. Several times during junior high, her friends shunned her. Like all kids her age, she went through some painful interpersonal experiences. To avoid that pain and anxiety, Stephanie retreated into her academic world where she had far more control.

At school, home and church, Stephanie was driven from within to be the best she could be. When asked about her greatest ambition, she immediately replied, "I always want to be the best I can be at whatever I do." Stephanie's self-esteem and identity were balanced on her personal evaluation of her performance in all areas of her life.

▶ Unhealthy Forms of the Power-Oriented Personality

When teenagers use their power-oriented defenses excessively, they lose the positive benefits of security their defense mechanisms have worked for. Their behavior becomes unhealthy, and their interpersonal relationships suffer. Their attitudes, behaviors and perceptions of others become rigid and unyielding. As the pattern continues, these young people begin to lose touch with their world's reality. Stephanie is a good example of someone whose increasing rigidity was slowly leading her to a poor adaptation in her adolescent world.

In this section we'll examine two more case studies: the "dictator" and the "perfectionist." Both these power-oriented teenagers represent unhealthy extremes of this personality type.

The Dictator. As a young child, Cynthia's two older brothers and their friends repeatedly teased and tormented her. She felt terribly alone and outnumbered. She had few opportunities to play with other children since in her neighborhood there was only one other small child, a little girl two years younger than Cynthia. Both her parents worked full time, and there was little time to relax together as a family. Her parents accomplished most of the shopping, errands and other household chores on the weekends, leaving Cynthia to again defend herself from her brothers and their friends.

Cynthia learned early she had to be responsible for her own life and well-being. She also learned that when she wasn't in control of her life and those around her, she was vulnerable. For her, being vulnerable meant getting hurt and being helplessly angry.

Cynthia took to school what she learned at home. In each class she was confronted with 25 to 30 people who might take advantage of her. She started each school year restricting her friendships to only those children who allowed her to control the relationship. This pattern continued throughout junior high and into high school. Although she was reasonably well-liked and respected, most girls couldn't get close to her. Those who did soon found that everything had to go her way, which wasn't always negative. Cynthia had good ideas. She knew how to have fun, and she did nice things for her friends. It's just that she always had to maintain control.

Since her last year of junior high and through high school, Cynthia's home life was turbulent. One of her brothers moved out. Her other brother and both parents resented her efforts to control things at home. Tremendous power struggles developed. Raised voices and flaring tempers reflected the tension. Her parents wondered if she'd ever learn to compromise and work with other people.

Cynthia experienced similar problems at church. She responded well to the thought of serving others. But she interpreted being a servant similar to the way a dominant, authoritarian man interprets what it means to be "head of the household." For Cynthia, serving meant to chair a committee, direct a project, lead a group or teach a class. Her interpretation of serving always incorporated being in charge of what was happening.

Cynthia's rigid demand for control increasingly limited her interpersonal effectiveness and fulfillment. She didn't allow people close to her to grow and mature in their ability to take care of themselves. She felt threatened, insecure and afraid when others tried to lead. To dispel her anxiety, she automatically sought to regain control of the situation.

The dictator is obviously an extreme of the leader. There's rarely ill intent in the dictator's heart. Behavior such as Cynthia's is motivated more by fear, pain, anxiety and sometimes anger. This young person's intensity rises merely as an attempt to protect his or her own sense of security.

The Perfectionist. Vincent was born in the

United States a few years after his parents immigrated from an Asian country. They lived in an ethnic neighborhood in a West Coast city. His father was an engineer, and his mother owned and managed a small restaurant.

Vincent's parents sought counseling for him when he developed severe obsessions about germs and the persistent fear that he'd lost his salvation. He also engaged in compulsive hand washing and other useless repetitive actions. His counselor began working with him during the last semester of his senior year.

Vincent was an only child raised in a tightly structured, well-ordered home. The dominant parent was his mother, though both parents loved him very much. Vincent was an easy child to raise. He obeyed his parents, required little correction and completed his chores with minimum reminding. Vincent continued to be a conscientious, successful student. In his church youth group Vincent emerged as a leader, willing to give much time and energy to that ministry. Throughout his adolescence he exhibited few signs of outward rebellion. Family friends considered his parents fortunate to raise such a fine son.

Early in life Vincent learned how to get his parents' and other adults' approval. He learned to give them what he thought they wanted from him. He offered academic excellence, proper manners, correct behavior and acceptance of responsibility as continual insurance for approval and praise.

During elementary school Vincent committed his life to Christ. He sought God's approval the same way he gained approval from other authority figures. Hard work and diligent efforts served Vincent well until his last semester of high school when he began suffering from his demand for personal perfection.

Being perfect was the one way Vincent could gain visible, tangible proof of parental approval and God's acceptance. This concern about God's acceptance, mixed with deep personal guilt, caused his defense system to crack.

One special relationship contributed significantly to Vincent's feeling unacceptable. The summer before his senior year, Vincent dated a girl he'd been attracted to for several months. By the summer's end, they were involved in fre-

quent petting sessions, sometimes engaging in manual stimulation of her genitals. After those experiences, Vincent felt
extreme guilt. He feared his parents would be crushed if
they found out what he'd done, and he was sure he'd disappointed God too. He also fell short of his own ideals. Vincent based his perfection on maintaining perfect self-control.
The act of partially giving in to his sexual desires represented a breach in his strong ability to control his impulses.

As with so many perfectionists, Vincent's guilt expressed
itself in a self-punishing manner. With each new pimple and
occasional cold sore, he was obsessed with a fear he'd contracted some type of venereal disease. Positive his sin would
somehow result in punishment, one obsession led to
another. And soon Vincent was hopelessly involved in a
complex maze of obsessions and compulsions such as the
repetitive hand washing mentioned earlier.

Perfectionists are tyrants demanding absolute perfection
primarily from themselves. They willingly respond to their
own command to be perfect but, like Vincent, don't understand that only through God's grace can perfection be
given.

► Effects of Power-Oriented Behavior on Others

Each of the eight personality types in this book have developed different interpersonal defense mechanisms. These
defensive strategies are designed to help the individual avoid
anxiety. Since each personality type strives for personal
comfort and security differently, each defense system has a
different effect on others. Power-oriented behavior usually
elicits one of two responses.

• Respect. Confidence, assertiveness and strong self-
control are attractive to other young people who secretly
wish they could be sure of themselves. A young person
who functions effectively with a power facade becomes a
hero worthy of high esteem. Dependency is gladly given to
one who appears better qualified to face life. In fact, other
young people often feel safer when they depend on someone else's strength rather than their own.

• Negative reactions. Even when other teenagers are comfortable with their dependency, they may become angry and resistive if the power-oriented teenager controls or dominates too much. Common reactions include resistance, rebellion or even withdrawal.

The effective "leader" draws admiration and trust from other adolescents. Many yield to his or her advice and decisions. The "brain" certainly elicits awe and respect. In fact, most teenagers feel inferior to a peer with these competencies. Others' inferiority feelings then widen the interpersonal gap and increase the power-oriented teenager's security, importance and competence.

The "dictator" draws anger, frustration and resentment from most adolescent peers. Teenagers act out these unpleasant feelings in rebellion and withdrawal. Only the most dependent adolescents tolerate being dominated to such an extent. A "perfectionist" normally elicits only frustration and lack of understanding from his or her peers. Friends who would like to help are kept at a distance. Only the perfectionist can help himself or herself.

A power-oriented teenager views others as weak and less capable than they really are. This error in perception is one more way this teenager seeks to reinforce his or her own sense of personal value and importance.

▶ Guidelines for Parenting Power-Oriented Adolescents

Parents have a potentially greater impact on their children than anyone else. This is both a frightening and inspiring reality. We're unnerved as we observe our children emulating some of our less attractive personal traits. Yet we're inspired to higher levels of personal responsibility by the challenge to "train a child in the way he should go" (Proverbs 22:6a). Each adolescent personality type in this book provides unique parenting tasks and opportunities. Parents need to learn how to adapt their parenting styles to the personality needs of each of their children. This section offers suggestions specifically designed for parenting power-oriented adolescents.

1. Look beyond your teenagers' actions to the meaning expressed in their behavior. It's dangerously easy during the pressures of

everyday family living to react unthinkingly to our teenagers' behaviors. We must consciously ask ourselves, "What
are they telling me by the way they act?" Remember, pre-
adolescent children usually express their feelings and attitudes more freely through actions than words. Though
adolescents have developed a greater capacity for verbalizing
their emotions and perceptions, they still act out their inner
tensions and conflicts through behavior.

Become a careful observer of your children's behavior.
Look for patterns and repetitive actions. Check with your
teenagers about the accuracy of your thoughts concerning
their actions. Realize their first responses may not be completely accurate or even honest. By using careful observation, patient listening and sensitive probing, you can gain a
much clearer picture of what their behavior actually means.

Careful observation may indicate that your power-oriented
young people demand perfection in almost everything they
do. Note their patterns, and then gently check with your
teenagers on what they mean by their behavior. Use these
opportunities to help them deal with their actions' underlying cause.

"Bill, I've noticed that when we have family discussions
you usually speak not only for yourself but also for your
brother and sister. I think they're getting upset about it. I
wasn't sure if you were aware of what was happening. What
does your 'taking over for them' do for you?"

Understand that behavior is one of the most important
avenues through which teenagers express their developing
identities. By paying close attention to their actions, you can
learn a tremendous amount about who they are.

**2. Provide opportunities for your teenagers to experience their
strength in beneficial ways.** God has blessed these young people with certain gifts and abilities. Help them find even more
ways to develop their strength. Assist them in utilizing their
gifts in ways that benefit others and themselves. Research
tells us that people are most likely to make positive personal
changes when they feel positive about themselves. You can
help your young people feel good about themselves by ac-
knowledging their positive characteristics. As their self-
esteem rises, power-oriented teenagers are more capable and

willing to risk the hard work of making personal changes.

Provide opportunities for your teenagers to exercise strength and leadership at home with the family. Let them lead or moderate family discussions. Give them responsibilities such as organizing and putting on Dad's 45th birthday party or planning part of the family vacation this summer. Give them increasing responsibility for younger children when appropriate. Gradually include them and their thoughts in making family financial decisions.

When your power-oriented teenagers assert strength and leadership, reinforce their positive efforts and behavior. Let them know you appreciate their decision-making abilities and strength to take charge of a situation. Make sure they know you admire their persuasive skills and ability to lead group activities.

3. Gently confront your teenagers' excessive use of power. Young people don't automatically know how to use their strengths. They must learn the appropriate exercise of power. Teenagers need supportive correction rather than criticism. When parents misinterpret power-oriented teenagers' strengths to mean security and self-assurance, they forget that their teenagers' presentations of power are defenses against feelings of insecurity. Therefore, harsh, demeaning or critical correction can cause extensive psychological damage without the adolescents letting anyone know they're hurting. Remember, excessive use of power often suggests internal conflict, insecurity or low self-esteem.

Instead of confronting your power-oriented teenagers, help them recognize their excessive uses of power. You can guide your young people as they search for other ways to handle interpersonal situations.

"Tom, I've noticed that when you're with your friends you push extremely hard for what you want to do. I wonder how your friends would feel if you sometimes asked them what they'd like to do."

"Charlotte, at the party last night you didn't seem satisfied with how others wanted to decorate the room. I wonder if your friends get tired of always having to do things your way."

As parents, you're in a critical position to gently guide

your adolescents to recognize and alter their power-oriented ways of relating in social situations.

4. Help your teenagers learn to work with others, not control them. Power-oriented teenagers find a sense of security in social relationships when they operate in leadership roles or from other prominent positions. They feel safe in these roles because they feel competent and self-reliant. However, their own self-sufficiency insulates them from the social contact and interpersonal intimacy they need. When you see your teenagers seeking positions of control, power and influence over others, encourage them to accept and recognize their friends and peers as equals. This recognition helps them develop a healthier balance in their own personality development.

These young people need to experience working with other family members to accomplish family goals. They need to know they can be treated like their brothers or sisters without losing their personal value. They need to share a wide variety of family experiences such as working in the yard or helping with housekeeping chores, in a capacity that doesn't make them special. Picking up dog droppings, pulling weeds and cleaning toilet bowls are unpleasant tasks, but they don't lessen the personal value of the teenagers who do them. On the contrary, willingness to participate in these jobs indicates that adolescents are learning the art of serving others.

Structure chores and projects so that your power-oriented adolescents work equally with or serve under another's supervision. Follow these experiences with discussions about feelings. Have the whole family tell how they feel about working together. Mutual experiences and family talks may open doors for each person to recognize the others' value.

5. Encourage your teenagers to recognize and value others' strengths. Often in their efforts to focus continually on their own sufficiency, perfection and strength, these young people either fail to see or actively avoid recognizing other family members' strengths and leadership abilities. They may feel threatened and lose some self-esteem when a brother, sister or parent takes control of a situation. When another family member displays his or her expertise, power-oriented teenagers may withdraw or assert their strengths even more forcefully. Those who're better adapted socially feel less threatened when another family member takes charge. However, those who are less secure may need help to offer others respect without losing their own self-respect.

You can help your power-oriented children see how they benefit from others' strengths. Point out how the athletic games they star in would be less exciting without the pep band's musical abilities. Help your strong academician appreciate the skills and talents of the mechanics who keep his or her car running. Use your family as an illustration of the body of Christ presented in Romans 12:3-8. Celebrate each person's "different gifts" in a Bible study that focuses on these verses. Then have family members each either write on a piece of paper or tell one another the strengths they benefit from or admire in the others. Recognizing and showing appreciation for one another's value helps develop self-esteem without encouraging power or control of others.

6. Teach these young people the value of deferring to others' leadership. After power-oriented teenagers can recognize another's strength, their next step is to follow the lead of someone who's superior in a certain skill or talent. Help power-oriented teenagers experiment with choosing to defer to others. They need to discover through personal experience that they can retain their respect and value, even after allowing another to lead.

Another factor that makes deference so difficult for power-oriented adolescents is their inability to accept anything less than perfection in themselves. Deferring to another can mean dependence on that person. Power-oriented young people fear and avoid dependency at all costs because they perceive it as a weakness.

Power-oriented teenagers are accustomed to and even encourage others' dependency on them because another's dependence makes them feel more valued and important. Eldest brothers and sisters commonly and naturally experience positions where others depend on them. Younger siblings may need guidance about school and social relationships. They may need an older sibling's protection against the neighborhood bully. They may seek their older brother's or sister's advice about how to dress and how to attract the opposite sex. Parents often rely on their power-oriented children's strengths to help them with parenting or household tasks.

Power-oriented teenagers need help learning how to depend comfortably on others. Continually reassure these adolescents of your love and admiration for them even when you choose to depend on another family member's skills. Arrange things so your power-oriented adolescents have to rely on another's leadership. Put someone else in charge of driving the car or leading the family hike. Reinforce your teenagers' dependency and any expression of a positive attitude when this response occurs.

"Sometimes it's nice not to be in charge, isn't it?"

"It's fun to let your little brother lead the way for a change, don't you think?"

"Sue, I like the way you let your younger sister design the menu for tonight's meal. I bet it was tough to sit back and let her take the lead!"

These young people gain the ability to balance their relationships as they learn to defer leadership to others.

7. Encourage these teenagers to accept their weaknesses. Power-oriented young people are usually quite intolerant of any weaknesses they find in themselves. Their affinity to power is their primary defense against their humiliation when they encounter personal inadequacies. Their greatest fear is that others will discover their weaknesses.

Effective parenting includes helping these teenagers accept their internal weaknesses. They need to know that weakness is an integral aspect of every human being. It's our inherent weakness that ultimately leads us to our greatest blessing, God's love through Jesus Christ. Our weaknesses also lead us into interdependent relationships with others in the body of Christ.

Lead the way for your children to learn a healthy attitude toward their personal weaknesses. Accept your own inadequacies, and exercise patience as you seek to grow. Practice admitting weaknesses and faults so your confessions come with greater ease. Be willing to confess your own weaknesses to your adolescents and do so without a self-demeaning pretense.

When you observe a weakness or fault in your young people, express a non-judgmental spirit of acceptance.

"Jayne, that's okay. We've all broken crystal or china or something else of value."

"Dave, I know flunking your driving test depressed you. Let's talk about it and see what you need to study. Then we can go out and get something to eat."

Acknowledge your teenagers' feelings. Let them know you think they're okay, even with their weaknesses. Then encourage them to move on.

8. Encourage your young people to value their own thinking.

Power-oriented teenagers need help to respond to internal reinforcement rather than others' praise. Most dominant adolescents were either heavily praised for their strengths or discouraged for asserting themselves during their childhood. The apostle Paul, in his letter to the Ephesian church, warned, "Fathers, do not exasperate your children . . ." (Ephesians 6:4). Frustrating or exasperating children's assertions of their identity causes difficulty with their attitudes about dominance and authority. Experiences of too much praise or excessive discouragement teach teenagers to be extremely sensitive to how others react to them.

Encourage your power-oriented adolescents to trust and value their own thinking. When asked what you think, you could respond: "I know you want me to tell you what I think, but I bet you have some good ideas. I'd like to hear what you've thought about first. Then if I have an additional idea, I'll tell it to you."

9. Encourage your teenagers to gradually expand their comfort boundaries.

Most of us tend to operate where we feel comfortable. We like the familiar. Situations and activities that previously offered success, accomplishment and acceptance are what we like to spend most of our time and effort doing. Power-oriented children like to stay with activities that make them feel like an expert. Concentrating on a particular area of academic study, playing a musical instrument, participating in one or more sports activities, working on cars, experiencing a hobby and developing an extensive social life are common areas of adolescent interest.

Encourage your teenagers' interests in their areas of strength. Then help them find and explore other avenues of self-expression. Understand that broadening personal interests represents taking a risk for power-oriented adolescents. To venture into something new means starting as a novice. Point out that enjoyment and personal satisfaction are just as important, if not more so, than attaining a certain level of perfection. Call their attention to the pleasures they experience in doing something, whether or not they do it particularly well.

"Even though you're not a concert pianist, it's still fun to play."

"I know school is difficult for you, Bob. But how are you doing at making your studies more interesting?"

You enrich your power-oriented children's lives when you help them expand their horizons. Their insecurities may cause them to resist your efforts to help, but patiently and gently encourage and reinforce their efforts.

10. Let your teenagers know it's okay to accept God's grace, and others' help and grace. Power-oriented teenagers usually have difficulty with the concept of grace. It's important to help these young people intellectually grasp and actively accept God's grace, for it can bring deep healing to them, both psychologically and spiritually. But these teenagers have a twofold problem with this task:

• First, relying on God's grace means trusting something other than their own expertise, strength and perfection.

• Second, relying on God's grace means becoming dependent on God and admitting the insufficiency of their own strength. They must admit they need God.

Both these tasks are required if we're to accept God's freely given grace. Power-oriented adolescents have an especially difficult time overcoming their resistance to grace. The apostle Paul wrote, "I can do everything through him who gives me strength" (Philippians 4:13). The teenagers described in this chapter respond readily to the first part of this verse. However, they seem to overlook the last phrase. "I can do everything . . ." becomes the ideal they strive for. But, "through him who gives me strength" suggests they aren't completely sufficient for the task. These phrases correctly suggest reliance on a source of strength other than their own.

Christ says, "Be perfect, therefore, as your heavenly Father is perfect" (Matthew 5:48). These young people respond readily to the call, but seek perfection under the cruel illusion that they can reach this goal with their own strength. They honestly believe they can reach perfection in themselves. They don't know yet how to respond to Christ's invitation found later in Matthew: "Come to me, all you who are weary and burdened, and I will give you rest. Take my yoke upon you and learn from me, for I am gentle and humble in heart, and you will find rest for your souls. For my yoke is easy and my burden is light" (Matthew 11:28-30). As parents, we can show power-oriented young people how to find the psychological and spiritual rest Christ promises by helping them understand and rely on God's grace.

Along with difficulty accepting God's grace, power-oriented teenagers don't easily accept others' help or assistance. To receive others' support, especially peers', alerts these adolescents to their inadequacies. "If I accept help from you, then I admit I'm incompetent."

Parents frequently observe their power-oriented children resisting others' offers to help. "No, that's all right. I can handle it myself. I've got it under control."

Sometimes resistance becomes firmer. "No. It's not necessary for you to help. I'm doing just fine, thank you."

When teenagers feel especially threatened, their resistance sounds hostile or aggressive. "No, I don't need your help! If I need it, I'll ask for it!" "I'm sorry you think I'm so stupid! Maybe if you back off, you'll see I can handle things at least as well as you can."

One of the most effective ways you can help these young people is by modeling a gracious acceptance of help when it's offered. This is particularly powerful when power-oriented teenagers are the ones offering the assistance. "Alice, thank you so much. I can use all the help I can get." Show your power-oriented adolescents that everyone gains when someone helps another. Help them see that everyone needs to know that he or she can help somebody else. Let them know they don't lose any stature or personal significance because they periodically need assistance. Finally, help them recognize that as part of Christ's body, they can't be self-sufficient; they'll always require the other believers' support.

These young people resist accepting others' help because their needs make them feel more inadequate than others. They feel guilty about needing help. Your support and acceptance of their needs can make a significant difference in their ability to grow in accepting others' help and support.

God promises his presence in all life's struggles—through good and bad times. With his help, parents can help their power-oriented adolescents accept their imperfections and grow to personal acceptance in a supportive environment.

CHAPTER TWO

The Competitive Personality

Most adolescents are competitive. Teenagers constantly compare themselves with others because of their strong peer-orientation. Comparing and competing are essential to their identity formation, for no one can determine who he or she is while living in a void.

Some teenagers become excessively competitive. Rather than compete normally as part of their development, they choose competition as their primary way of relating to others. They also adopt this method as their main defense for warding off anxiety and insecurity.

Narcissism is another normal part of the adolescent personality. Psychologists say people are narcissistic when they:
• have a hard time seeing a perspective other than their own,
• are idealistic and exaggerate their self-evaluations,
• can love only themselves,
• perceive everything in light of what's good for them, and
• exert most of their efforts toward benefiting themselves.

We identify teenagers as having a competitive personality when their desire for competition and their narcissism become extreme. These young people's competitive defenses characterize the way they interact with everyone. They feel comfortable only when they see themselves as better than others. While power-oriented teenagers need to feel competent and in control, competitive teenagers must feel superior to others.

Competitive adolescents abhor dependency. Yet in a surprisingly ironic way, they strongly depend on others. Without a standard for comparison, these teenagers have no way to establish their self-esteem. They depend on seeing others as inferior. What difficulty these young people have with Paul's admonition: "Let us not become conceited, provoking and envying each other." "Each one should test his own actions. Then he can take pride in himself, without comparing himself to somebody else, for each one should carry his own load" (Galatians 5:26; 6:4-5).

Competitive teenagers engage in activities that reinforce their perception of being better than others. They strive for perfection to further enhance their sense of superiority. They seek power over others to make others feel inferior. While the power-oriented teenager's motto is, "I need to be the best I can possibly be," the competitive teenager believes, "I need to be better than you."

► Development of the Competitive Personality

Many factors that produce power-oriented personalities also develop competitive personalities. Power is important to both types of young people. The use of that power differentiates these two types of teenagers. While power-oriented adolescents use power to develop skills for their own maturation and growth, competitive adolescents employ power against others to enhance themselves. Several factors influence the competitive personality's development.

1. High energy levels. Since competition requires continuous striving, these adolescents require a capacity for hard-driving power and vigorous action. Adequate nourishment and rest are essential. Physical weakness and low energy denote inadequacy, which is unacceptable to the competitive teenager.

2. Competitive parents or guardians. Children assume many of the behaviors they see in their parents. Parents who regularly criticize the pastor, demean their neighbors or talk disparagingly about school and government officials train their teenagers to do the same. These patterns assume particular significance when other family members also compete with one another. These teenagers grow up believing this interaction style is normal for relating in families and to others.

3. Positive reinforcement. Whether the competition is in athletics, academics, popularity, wealth or even spirituality, our social system provides worthwhile rewards to the winners. Athletic success brings attention and respect. Academic excellence earns adult approval and scholarships. Wealth attains power, prestige, possessions and peers' attention. Outstanding spiritual behavior elicits approval from adults and the Christian community. These desirable reinforcements increase teenagers' competitive behavior.

4. Pain and discomfort while under someone else's control. Severe or overly punitive parents have taught these young people the dangers of operating under another person's direction. Like power-oriented young people, competitive teenagers experience this hurt and decide they must maintain control of themselves and others. But competitive teenagers go beyond this decision. They use power to deprive others of any vestige of strength and then employ this control to ensure their own supremacy.

5. Distrust of others, especially others who have power. Unhappy or negative experiences with power figures have taught these young people not to get close to others. Since adolescence is also a time of high idealism and critical thinking, this combination of factors leads to self-righteousness and a strong critical attitude toward authority. Newspaper headlines and TV newscasts about dishonesty and corruption in government, schools and churches reinforce adolescents' distrust of others. Competitive teenagers believe the way to protect themselves is by preventing others from having power over them and possessing power over others.

6. Self-distrust. Some competitive teenagers become aware of their own imperfections and tendencies to mistreat others. Other competitive teenagers may recognize their misuse of power. Still others may distrust their abilities to maintain control. They feel driven to work harder and harder to maintain control. Compulsively, these teenagers seek more and more power, hoping to somehow find security and psychological comfort.

Most competitive teenagers have several of these six causative factors in their background. Identifying these conditions helps us understand much of their behavior's meaning.

► *Healthy Forms of the Competitive Personality*

In our culture, competition is highly valued and occurs in almost every interpersonal arena. Teenagers who develop a competitive personality can be successful during their adolescence. They can establish interpersonal habits that will serve them well through adulthood. The keys to a healthy adaptation through competition are moderation and balance. Let's look at some healthier forms of the competitive personality.

The Politician. Political activity is a socially approved avenue for competition. It allows politicians to develop strategies, motivate people and gain popularity. Politics provide adolescent competitors with immediate, tangible feedback. Politicians either win or lose. Winners receive rewards of control, power and supremacy over others. Losers experience the pain of defeat and an unsettling reminder of their lack of power, loss of control and feelings of inferiority.

Randy is a high school junior. He's deeply involved in his campaign to be next year's student-body president. If he wins, he'll have accomplished one of his fondest dreams. This goal represents the culmination of his extracurricular activities since elementary school. Randy's social involvement in school has primarily involved various kinds of political activities. He's helped friends run for office, competed in his own political races and campaigned for social and humanitarian causes.

As the fifth of six children in a home where both parents work, Randy learned early how to get his needs met. His four older sisters were delighted to have a younger brother. Each experimented with the "Mommy" role, competing for his attention. He gladly entered the drama, intensifying their competition for his benefit. Randy quickly and happily became irretrievably spoiled.

Then along came baby brother. Randy lost his position at

the center of his family's universe and was replaced by an unexpected and unwanted (at least unexpected and unwanted by Randy!) baby boy. Suddenly, after 10 years of receiving everyone's special attention, Randy was expected to give. Randy had met his first competitor.

During his early childhood Randy learned how to pressure, entice and manipulate others to do his bidding. During elementary school he extended his technique to include his classmates. He felt comfortable when he controlled the playground action. However, when he wasn't the team captain, he felt uneasy and awkward. Whatever the interpersonal setting, Randy needed to be in control.

Throughout his school years Randy's classmates respected and admired him. Gradually, he became selective of the activities he joined in with his friends. He chose only situations in which he could quickly ascend to a leadership position. In the process of gaining control, he caused others to feel inferior. He subtly manipulated them into believing he should be their leader. They accepted his efforts toward leadership as beneficial to their needs and gladly helped him attain that position.

As Randy progressed through junior high and into high school, he involved himself in other activist types of events. He organized and led student campaigns against poverty and social injustice. He coordinated students' efforts to pressure teachers and administrators to give them more benefits such as campus vending machines and longer lunch periods. He gained popularity, attention and respect from his peers and adults for his efforts. As effective as he was, he continually judged and criticized his peers' leadership efforts and put them down when they weren't successful. He saw himself as superior, but soon learned he lost others' respect and support if he allowed them to see his demeaning attitude toward them.

Randy opened many doors of opportunity for himself through his competitive political activities. He met and interacted with more people than he would have otherwise, but his competitive stance kept others at a distance. His automatic faultfinding and continual search for others' weaknesses made people around him uneasy. With each new meeting Randy worked to reaffirm his position of superiority.

The Jock. From the time he was born, Spence was a great delight to his father. An outstanding high school athlete and average college competitor, his dad had hoped Spence would earn a position on a professional basketball team. But his height prevented his being a serious contender. Helping his son accomplish athletic goals he hadn't achieved became a driving force for this highly competitive father.

As Spence reached the third grade, his dad encouraged his participation in Little League baseball and soccer. When he was finally old enough, his father enrolled him in the children's community basketball league. Fortunately, Spence was naturally agile and had excellent eye-hand coordination. He quickly grasped the game's basic skills and improved rapidly.

Spence's athletic activities were obviously valuable to his father who attended all Spence's games and most of his practices. When he was with Spence in the car or at home, he centered their conversations on sports. Even his church attendance was regulated by "important" games in town or on television. Spence's father obviously avoided school open-house activities, board games and other non-sports activities, which let Spence know his father's priorities.

As Spence grew up, he learned how to get his dad's attention and approval. Spence received his father's positive reinforcement for competing and succeeding in all sports. However, if Spence performed poorly, let his interest or intensity lag or chose to do something else, his father made his disapproval obvious and at times even punished him. In an important sense Spence had to vie for his father's attention and love. He learned that his dad's acceptance of him was conditional on Spence's interest and active participation in sports and his ability to win.

Spence's experience with his father taught him he had to compete for personal significance. After all, how much personal value could he have if he had to repeatedly earn his own father's respect and esteem? He believed the myth that his personal value depended on his ability to compete with others on the playing field. Spence was unaware that he was having to compete with his father's needs to experience his own personal value.

Spence generalized what he'd learned from his relationship with his father to other relationships. When he lost any athletic competition, he felt a loss in self-esteem. Winning increased the value of his personal stock in himself. But there were always new competitions, and each one brought a new threat of losing personal worth.

Under the circumstances, Spence is now making a healthy adjustment to adolescence. His mother provides a stabilizing influence in his life. She loves and admires him whether he participates in sports or not. And she accepts him, regardless of whether he wins or loses.

Spence's competitive stance toward his peers is primarily visible in his attitude about himself. Even though he's kind and friendly toward others, there's an underlying, inner tension that prevents his relaxing and enjoying himself completely. A constant, though often unconscious, need to be better than those around him pervades his self-presentation. He feels he must be superior to others, or he jeopardizes his value and lovableness.

The Entrepreneur. Everyone at church knows Marcus. He's delightful, mischievous, charming and a bundle of energy! If you have a problem, Marcus has an angle. If you're down, he makes you smile. He can talk you into anything. Everybody loves Marcus!

Nothing gets Marcus down. He's always happy and energetic. His obvious enthusiasm for life surprises people when they hear about his background.

Marcus is one of six children. His father is an alcoholic. The family never had enough money for food, let alone adequate clothing and household necessities. There was never money for entertainment. His dad was a good machinist, but because of his drinking he worked an average of only two days per week. When Marcus was 9 years old, his father disappeared and was never heard from again. The family lived on welfare, plus whatever the children earned mowing lawns and babysitting and what their mother earned cleaning houses.

Throughout elementary school Marcus was quiet, shy and embarrassed about his appearance. Normally, he went unnoticed, except for some mild teasing about his clothes. He was a nice kid, but nobody paid much attention to him. During junior high, he became friends with members of a church youth group. After attending several meetings, Marcus made a personal commitment to Christ. He felt accepted by this friendly, caring group. He lost his initial shyness and guarded mistrust. He excitedly joined in their activities and became a regular group member.

Even though he was accepted and enjoyed by the other kids, Marcus still felt different from them. He felt he must always strive for their acceptance. He continually needed reassurance that he really was a member and belonged. Since Marcus was and still is an active boy, he didn't wait for reassurances to come to him. Instead, he went out and earned them. Marcus carved his own niche in the youth group. He became an idea man with enough energy to not only create schemes, but put them into action.

Marcus became a whiz at dreaming up creative fund raisers. With his ability to advertise activities plus the active support of the youth group members and their parents, he'd make almost any project an outstanding success. With his enthusiasm and organizational skills, the youth group raised money for summer and winter camps, a new youth room Ping-Pong table and a summer canoe trip. Other special projects produced Christmas gifts for orphanage children and elderly residents at a convalescent home.

Marcus also earned a reputation for being an entrepreneur for his own sake. During the past year he gained control of six paper routes. He paid younger children a percentage to deliver for him, and he made the collections. In addition, he hired himself out to school clubs as a fund raiser. He produced the ideas, directed the projects and pocketed 25 percent of the profits.

As an entrepreneur, Marcus earned a popular, valuable place both at school and in youth group. He receives reinforcement repeatedly for his creative and energetic efforts. But for Marcus, there's never enough affirmation. An empty feeling almost immediately follows each success, driving him to devise new, more elaborate schemes to prove his worth to his group. When others come up with ideas, Marcus has to have a better one. When others work hard, Marcus puts out more effort. When others are charming, Marcus virtually oozes social appeal.

Beneath his energetic, spontaneous and charming exterior, Marcus feels unsure of his social value. He questions how much people would like him if he didn't try so hard. When others begin doing what he does, he feels threatened. His competitive response reconfirms his position as best at what he does and provides Marcus his only security.

Randy, Spence and Marcus are all competitive teenagers. They depend on seeing themselves as better than their peers for self-esteem and personal value. In their minds they secure their belonging by establishing their superiority over others. Even though all three believe dependence on others is an insecure, dangerous position, these competitive adolescents express their basic defense in a healthy, constructive manner to themselves and those around them.

► Unhealthy Forms of the Competitive Personality

Some competitive teenagers aren't as well-adjusted as Randy, Spence and Marcus. They compete with such strong insecurity that they're destructive to themselves and others. Their intense competitiveness ruins relationships, and they're unbearable to be around for more than a short time.

The Snob. Marsha obviously has a difficult time getting along with others. At age 19, she never has had a good friendship for more than a few months. Few people can tolerate her self-centeredness. There's no room in her life for anyone but herself. Throughout her childhood Marsha was spoiled with excessive attention, immediate response to her every whim and the fulfillment of most every material wish. Marsha was indeed spoiled . . . spoiled rotten!

Marsha's extravagant and indulgent upbringing also protected her from experiencing almost every uncomfortable or threatening situation. She wasn't expected to go to parties, activities or other social events where she might feel awkward or uneasy. Her parents treated her as "special" and told her she didn't have to mix with children who were "beneath" her. As a result, few social situations emerged in which Marsha felt at ease. She knew few peers she felt confident with, and her interpersonal world became increasingly troubled.

Marsha went through high school feeling like an outcast among her peers. She never learned how to adapt to their needs and wishes. Furthermore, if they didn't adjust to her demands, she withdrew from them, proudly pointing her nose in the air. Finally, she was forced to rely on her superior collection of material possessions for comfort. She had to look to her endless array of dresses, designer jeans and shoes for her self-confidence.

Her life experiences were also different from most of her peers'. Since her parents had plenty of money, they'd taken her on many exotic vacations. By the time Marsha graduated from high school, she'd visited Europe, Asia, Australia, the Caribbean and the Mediterranean. She still carries all these vacations and other unique experiences in her collection of proofs that she's better than her peers.

Superiority became her only way to feel important. She earned the nickname "Princess" among her fellow students. Her freshman year in college was deeply disappointing. Hoping to find friends there, she instead found herself relating in the same distancing manner she did in high school. By boasting about herself, she automatically put people off. And whenever anyone tried to get close to her, she became arrogant and offensive.

Tragically, Marsha has become a social cripple. She desperately wants to be included by her peers. She yearns for a best friend. And she can only imagine what it would be like to have a boyfriend. Her parents' lesson that she was "too special" to have to relate with other kids has limited her to the point that she feels isolated and different. Her deepening depression, periodic anxiety attacks and deteriorating academic performance caused her to leave college before the end of the semester. She's enlisted a professional counselor's help. Their mutual task is to release her from her prison of social isolation. Her once lofty and secure place of superiority has become her desolate cell of alienation. Marsha is so good at competing she's reached the top and found how lonely it can be.

The Macho Man. "Be tough, kid." "No son of mine is going to let himself be pushed around." "Make 'em respect you." "Don't take that kind of abuse from anybody." "Always treat girls with respect, but never let them forget who's boss." Herbert grew up enmeshed in his father's "wisdom." His dad's example and advice heavily impacted his view of himself, his world and other people. His father was dictator in their home, and his mother submitted to the role of faithful servant. Their children were to be "seen but not heard." The boys were taught to be macho, their dad's interpretation of masculinity, while Herbert's sisters were instructed to be feminine and submissive.

Like most children, Herbert desperately wanted to please his father. He practiced the "tough kid" routine daily. He learned not only how to walk, but how to "move." He presented himself powerfully, using a few well-chosen words and an aloof, superior attitude. He observed most people through an expressionless, masklike face and half-glazed eyes, giving the overall impression of superior indifference.

Herbert looked down on outstanding students, serious athletes or students heavily involved in organized activities as people too weak to stand on their own. Underlying this critical attitude was Herbert's unrecognized self-rejection for his inability to succeed in a more productive manner. With no parental support for success in academic studies, involvement in sports or participation in other school activities, Herbert neglected these areas of his life. This neglect surfaced during junior high when he was held back a year. In an effort to please his father, Herbert sealed his own fate by emulating his dad's critical attitudes toward those who seek excellence in traditional avenues. He periodically experienced fear, anxiety and panic that progress was leaving him behind. But these uncomfortable feelings quickly diminished when he renewed his efforts to prove himself the most macho guy around.

Herbert's competitive style works well for him in his neighborhood and at school. But there's little payoff for being macho at church. His mother attends church regularly and has always forced her children to attend with her. Upon reaching their teenage years, they're expected to become church youth group members. Though their dad's an occasional visitor on Christmas and Easter, he enforces their mother's wish that they go to church regularly. Herbert is regularly invited to participate in youth group discussions and special projects. Sometimes he overcomes his fears and apprehensions long enough to get involved. He allows himself a certain amount of enjoyment, but then withdraws when he feels his defenses dropping dangerously low.

Being a Christian poses difficult problems for Herbert. It requires him to depend on someone. It means he must be vulnerable and express love. These aspects of being Christian directly oppose his defensive style. Herbert can relate to trying to survive in the wilderness for 40 days, but he struggles intensely with washing another's feet.

The Sexual Tease. Delores is the youngest of three children. Her brothers are two and five years older than she. During their early adolescent years, both boys engaged in sexual play with her. Threatened into secrecy, Delores never revealed these activities to either brother nor anyone else. Intercourse was never accomplished, but both boys fondled her breasts and genitals. They also required her to stimulate them and demanded that she allow them to lie on top of her while naked. When these activities first occurred, Delores was frightened. However, she soon learned her brothers wouldn't hurt her, and gradually she began to experience pleasure too. This was about the only time either brother gave her any positive attention.

By the time Delores was 14 years old, these episodes had almost ceased. No one talked about them. Neither brother explained why they'd occurred or why he stopped. She merely assumed they'd lost interest in her. The cessation of their attention was okay with her. With the onset of puberty, she had feared she might get pregnant. Plus, she became increasingly resentful about their using her. Although it was pleasurable at times, she felt increasingly guilty and angry and vowed never to allow another boy to do those things to her.

These repeated molestations deeply affected Delores. During a crucial time in her identity development, she mistakenly learned her primary value to boys was as a sex object. Because of the excessive stimulation and arousal she had experienced, she began relating to her body mainly in terms of sexual function and pleasure. She also learned that sex can produce guilt; therefore, she felt a need to be secretive and deceitful.

Delores is now 16 years old and has had several short-term relationships with boys. She's quite seductive in her dress and movements. Boys stare and whistle. Behind her back girls talk about her with both envy and disdain. No one in the church youth group really knows Delores. She pulls away as soon as someone starts to get close. She isn't comfortable in close conversations and avoids them to subdue her rising anxiety level. She attracts boys with non-verbal suggestions that sexual activity is a good possibility. But she knows just when to cut them off. She's kept her personal vow to never again allow a boy to use her.

Her behavior pattern is circular. She needs affirmation and attention, so she presents a seductive come-on and attracts the attention she desires. The boy believes her message and responds sexually to her. Frightened and angry, Delores rejects him. With this rejection she reduces her anxiety level, reaffirms her belief that boys care only about sex and once again finds herself alone and needing attention. Delores' pattern is competitive in two ways. First, she competes with other girls to be the sexiest. Second, she competes and maneuvers to maintain constant control of boys.

► Effects of Competitive Behavior on Others

Interacting with others makes all of us uncomfortable at times. Competition is used by a teenager to make him or her more comfortable, confident and secure. Let's look at the effects this defensive style is designed to have on others.

A competitive teenager who moderates this defense can be effective in relationships. Other people often respond with respect, admiration and even awe.

"I could never do that."

"I don't see how she can possibly accomplish so much."

"How can he keep coming up with all those fantastic ideas?"

"I can't imagine being as good an athlete as he is."

Along with the high esteem other teenagers have for a competitive personality, they normally experience some degree of inferiority. Different from the responses initiated by the power-oriented personality, a competitive teenager stimulates low self-evaluations in others. A competitive adolescent relies heavily on making comparisons and feels valuable only when he or she seems superior.

As a competitive teenager becomes less healthy and struggles with his or her personal adjustment, behavior becomes more and more destructive in its effect on others. Sometimes exposure to a competitive adolescent provokes extreme self-rejection in peers.

"I'm not good enough."

"Next to him, I look stupid."

"If I'm competing against her, there's no reason for me to try. I'd look foolish for even thinking I might win."

Strong resentment and distrust are aroused. Since negative self-concepts are difficult and painful for teenagers to live with, many times these bad feelings are projected back to the competitive young person whose relationship stimulated these negative feelings. Unconsciously, the injured teenagers say, "Since my bad feelings get worse when I'm around you, I'm angry with you for making me feel so bad."

Not all teenagers respond to a competitive adolescent with submission; however, those who do often also experience anger, hurt and resentment. Other teenagers may commonly react to this personality type with jealousy, envy and suspicion. Keep this in mind: Other teenagers' personality types are also important factors in determining responses toward a competitive adolescent.

"Politicians" such as Randy often stimulate respect, suspicion or distrust in others. Typically, they can manipulate people to follow or submit. Adolescent "jocks" such as Spence usually inspire awe, admiration and envy. "Entrepreneurs" who operate like Marcus effectively elicit submission, agreement, following and trust from their peers.

We expect quite different reactions to "snobs" such as Marsha; they usually elicit envy, jealousy, resentment or anger from peers. "Macho men" such as Herbert gain envy and respect from some. In others, they stimulate anger, resentment and self-rejection. In addition to sexual attraction, "sexual teases" such as Delores often elicit envy, jealousy, distrust and self-depreciation. Observing how other young people respond to a teenager provides valuable clues for correctly identifying an adolescent's personality type. In addition, be aware of the response you and other adults have to your children.

▶ Guidelines for Parenting Competitive Adolescents

Competitive personalities present behavioral dynamics that run far deeper than normal adolescent competitiveness. These young people use brothers, sisters and especially parents as common targets for their competitive attitudes and actions. To effectively parent these adolescents, you must develop great patience, special understanding and specific skills. By following the suggestions in this section, you can help your competitive teenagers mature through their adolescent years toward a healthier and more fulfilling adulthood.

1. Learn to hear what your teenagers say about themselves through their behavior. When parents ask their teenagers why they did something, the reply is often, "I don't know." And most of the time, they're honest about their response. Your adolescents may be just as frustrated and confused about their behavior as you are. Many times they aren't conscious of the motivations behind their actions, nor are they aware of the goals their behavior is directed toward. By becoming better readers of your children's behavior, you learn much more about how they think and feel about themselves, their family and their world.

Sometimes you may find it difficult to control your spontaneous reactions to your competitive children long enough to gain an accurate understanding of what they're feeling. Seek to understand what events and circumstances contributed to their development of a competitive personality orientation. Look for experiences that might have damaged their development of a healthy self-esteem. Consider times they've been seriously demeaned or humiliated by important others.

Take special note of rejections and losses they've experienced in personal and family relationships.

Recognizing patterns of recurrent behavior is always more significant than noting individual incidents. Young people naturally experiment with new roles and try various ways to interact with their friends. They make mistakes, sometimes even serious errors that carry heavy consequences. However, you need to focus most of your attention on actions that are continually repeated.

2. Reinforce your teenagers' personal strength and encourage their growth in this area. Much of your competitive teenagers' security and okayness depends on their seeing themselves as not only strong, but stronger than others. Though this comparison is essentially unhealthy for building self-esteem, these adolescents must affirm their belief in their own adequacy before significant changes can occur. Let them know you recognize their talents and value their special abilities.

Show and tell your competitive teenagers that you appreciate their competency. Give them opportunities in your family and home to exercise their strengths. Place them in charge of certain household duties such as picking up the dry cleaning, planning the week's dinner menus or helping the younger children with their homework. Ask them to compose the family Christmas letter or coordinate and direct a younger sibling's birthday party. These are examples of tasks that may affirm your competitive teenagers' sense of adequacy if they accept and fulfill their responsibilities.

Helping your adolescents believe more fully in their strengths offers them a firm foundation to grow on. When you recognize and value their strengths, these young people feel less insecure about themselves. With less insecurity and anxiety, they can more accurately assess their needs to make personal changes.

3. Help your young people applaud others' strengths. Competitive teenagers' self-esteem is linked to their need to be on top. These young people struggle when their friends succeed and when others control situations they're involved in. Their self-confidence receives a shock when they see others receive credit for a job well-done. Their self-value diminishes when their friends are elected to leadership positions. These same reactions occur when others make the first-string squad ahead of them, when another is selected as a girlfriend or boyfriend in their place, when they think a brother or sister receives a better Christmas gift or when another is selected as the lead in the senior play instead of them. Competitive adolescents experience these situations as competitive events that they either win or lose.

Your children often learn their attitudes from watching you. Examine your reactions to others' successes and ask yourself how you respond to others' accomplishments. Do your teenagers observe your competitive attitudes? What kinds of reactions do they see when your friends and acquaintances make personal gains? Help your competitive teenagers by modeling a positive attitude toward others who succeed.

Affirm your teenagers' strengths, and guide them into positive responses toward others' successes. Encourage them to make a phone call or send a congratulatory card to a friend who's earned an honor. Or help them sponsor a party to celebrate the other person's achievement. No matter what response your teenagers choose, recognize their efforts to respond to another's success. When they realize others' accomplishments don't diminish their own value, they'll develop the personal strength to initiate these positive responses on their own.

4. Help your teenagers accept their weaknesses. Competitive teenagers develop their psychological defenses to protect themselves from the anxiety of feeling weak, incompetent or close to others. They develop their superior attitude to provide strength and distance themselves from others. These young people don't know they're okay without seeing themselves as the best. Their defensive needs cause them to constantly compare themselves with others. Then they draw their self-esteem and feelings of okayness directly from these comparisons.

To overcome extreme competitiveness, these teenagers need to develop the ability to accept their mistakes and their lack of certain talents. They'll need your help to accomplish this goal. Gently encourage your youthful competitors to admit their omissions, mistakes and inabilities. Model your own admissions of weakness. Let them see that you can maintain your self-respect. They need your example to know that recognizing and admitting one's personal faults doesn't result in a loss of personal dignity.

In addition to sharing your example with them, gently help these competitive adolescents recognize and admit their mistakes. Quickly assure them of your ongoing acceptance of and esteem for them. Let them know you don't see them as a lesser person. Help them understand that their willingness to become vulnerable actually causes you to respect them more. As they give you opportunities to accept, affirm and encourage them, your love and sensitivity toward them increase. "Denise, since you've opened up about how bad you feel when you do poorly, my love and respect for you have grown even more. It's like you're letting me get to know you more deeply." Competitive teenagers need to learn they don't become a lesser person when they recognize areas of personal inadequacy. By observing your modeling and hearing your affirmation, these teenagers gradually learn to do the same themselves.

5. Help your teenagers know they belong in your family because of who they are rather than because they're best at something. One of the most fundamental psychological needs children have is to know they belong. The family unit is the ideal environment in which to nurture this sense of belonging. Since competitive young people seek to secure their belonging by being better than others, they'll naturally compete with their brothers and sisters. Much of sibling rivalry relates to this competitive approach to securing a position within the family unit. By understanding the relationship between your teenagers' competitiveness and their need to belong, you can respond in ways that meaningfully meet your children's needs.

Help your children recognize and experience your love for who they are rather than what they do. Start simply by telling them that though their actions are important, you love them deeply, aside from what they do. Let them know that you love them as a gift from God. Tell your children that your love is separate from considerations about their behavior. Tell them that you value them as individuals created in God's image. Help them understand that God hasn't given them to you, but rather he's entrusted them to you for care and training.

Never put belonging in the family or your love for your children at risk during the discipline process. Don't use these relationships as rewards or punishments. Don't threaten your children with statements such as "If you don't stop that, I'm not going to love you anymore." For the sake of your teenagers' security, they must recognize your love and being part of their family as givens, not to be withdrawn under any circumstances.

6. Help your teenagers experience equality in relationships. Competitive adolescents feel comfortable and secure with others only when they're in a superior position. Relationships of equality typically produce anxiety within these teenagers. Equal relationships lack the superior-inferior role configuration that provides security for these young people. However, in order to function effectively in this world, these adolescents need to learn how to operate in equal and subordinate roles as well as superior roles. You can help your teenagers experience all these roles and feel comfortable in them.

Try using family meetings to make decisions and resolve

conflicts at home. Let each family member, including your competitive adolescents, have an equal say and vote in the final outcome. (As a general rule, only family members directly affected by the group's decision should be allowed to take part in the decision-making process. Also, in decisions where parental authority is an issue, a completely democratic approach may not be appropriate.) In most situations experiences as equal family members can benefit competitive adolescents. They may begin to feel closer to other family members and experience more connection with any final decisions.

Involve all family members in non-competitive play activities in which no one wins or loses. For example, bicycle, body surf, ski, swim, hike, backpack, watch television, go to the theater, listen to music, attend professional ball games and even fly kites. Playfulness usually relaxes individuals' defenses. When this relaxation occurs at home, competitive teenagers usually drop their defenses. Sharing equally in family responsibilities around the house or in the yard also provides these adolescents with opportunities for non-competitive family interaction.

The home environment is probably the safest place for competitive young people to explore equal relationships. As you present opportunities and involve them in these non-competitive family activities, ask them to tell how they feel about these experiences. Remember to listen to their responses and guide them to understand and work with their reactions.

7. Help your teenagers learn that dependence on others is acceptable and positive. Competitive young people feel unsafe and vulnerable when depending on a friend or an adult. When these teenagers aren't in a position of power or superiority, the close proximity of another person is unbearable for them. Dependency robs them of their superiority, which gives them their security.

Competitive teenagers prize their self-sufficiency so much that depending on another indicates personal failure or inadequacy. Another implicit reason these young people seek to avoid dependency is their lack of trust in others. Many of them fear others will use knowledge of their weaknesses and vulnerability against them.

The family is usually the best place to start helping competitive teenagers trust themselves and others more. Encourage your adolescents to begin taking risks by depending on other family members. You can take the first step by asking your teenagers for help. Depend on their strengths and talents, when appropriate. Ask their advice; then utilize their help. Ask for their suggestions when purchasing gifts for friends and relatives. Help them see that you depend on them when they help you carry in things from the car, help prepare meals, take over tasks in the yard and run errands for you. Express your sincere appreciation to them. Make sure they sense the relief and support you feel as a result of your depending on them. Explain to your competitive adolescents that everyone feels better when we mutually depend on one another. It feels just as good to have a burden lifted from our shoulders as it does to be able to help others.

Provide opportunities for you to help and support your competitive adolescents. Then try to get them to tell you how they felt when they received your help. Build nurturing and affirmation into your conversation with them.

"Thanks for letting me help you with your homework. You sure learn fast!"

"You did a good job overhauling your carburetor. I enjoyed helping."

These kinds of statements help your young people not to feel demeaned or devalued by your assistance.

Remember to point out how you see their friends helping one another. And direct your teenagers' attention to the same types of mutually helping relationships you see together on television or in movies.

Depending on others is a frightening experience for these competitive adolescents. Helping them gradually experience relying on others is one more step toward a healthier interpersonal style of relating for these young competitors.

8. Encourage these teenagers to gradually explore and expand the activities they feel competent in. Competitive teenagers consistently avoid the risk of being compared unfavorably with others. Since these young people need to feel superior to others, they usually restrict their activities to areas they feel competent in. They focus only on activities they can specialize in such as sports, academics, auto mechanics, a particular hobby, socializing, playing a musical instrument, acting, singing or setting up and operating audio-visual equipment. Venturing into other activities in which they lack knowledge or experience brings instant anxiety and panic, especially if others are observing.

This is another example of competitive teenagers' excessive focus on performance. They miss most of the pleasures found in whatever they do. Their focus on their performance's quality robs them of any personal or social enjoyment in the experience itself. These young people need to build enough self-confidence to allow them to enjoy their activities without being intensely preoccupied with evaluating their performance. They need to focus not on themselves, but on the activity or others who may be with them.

There are many things you can do to help your competitive teenagers grow out of this bind. Recognize that success, accomplishment and attaining perfection are extremely important to these adolescents. Take note of the areas in which your teenagers seem to have natural abilities. Are they skilled in music, sports, art, planning and organizing events or helping people who are sad? Select two or three areas in which your teenagers have yet to develop their talents and encourage their interests in these directions. Suggest ways to start and offer to participate with them. Play golf, tennis or some other leisure sport with each other. Encourage a total family activity that might stimulate your teenagers' interest in that activity. While your young people are trying something new, make comments that focus on enjoying the task rather than evaluating performance quality. "It sure is fun trying something new!" "I'm sure others can tell we're beginners, but let's not let that get in the way of having a good time."

Competitive teenagers need support to try activities they don't feel competent in. Helping them venture into new areas of interest lends much creativity and stimulation to their lives.

9. Help your teenagers gain a clearer understanding of how others think. In an effort to preserve their own security, competitive teenagers often shield themselves from knowing how other people perceive the world. They guard against knowing how other people think so they don't have to question their own perceptions, thoughts and attitudes. By isolating themselves, they maintain a comfortable void filled with only their own thoughts. Within this isolated sphere, only their own ways of perceiving the world and people exist.

The primary problem with this defensive structure is that it isolates the competitive adolescent from everyone else. These teenagers become rigid, casting aside everything that seems foreign to them. When confronted with a different thought, they usually try to deny its validity, argue against it or otherwise discredit it.

You can help your competitive teenagers lessen their negative reactions to other viewpoints, positions and thoughts. Initiate discussions of issues that don't have a right or wrong answer. Deciding whether a particular painting is attractive or whether a Ford is better than a Chevrolet are issues that can't be resolved with absolute yes or no answers. Ask your young people to tell you what they think another person's statement means. "What are the strong and weak points of Leslie's point of view?" "What did you understand Paul's point to be?" Reinforcing your teenagers for their perceptions' creativity and thoughtfulness can build their confidence in themselves as thinking people. As their self-confidence increases, other points of view threaten them less and less.

For competitive teenagers to become more mature in their world-view, they need the ability to consider and evaluate others' perceptions and thinking styles without feeling threatened. Your encouragement and affirmation as you participate with them in their struggle to understand others' thoughts and feelings can afford them invaluable help in this growth process.

10. Help your teenagers open themselves to their loving, tender feelings. These adolescents protect themselves from emotional vulnerability with their competitive defensive structure. By comparing themselves with others and maintaining a self-perception of superiority, they establish distance between themselves and others. They also protect themselves from the vulnerability that comes from contact with their soft, tender emotions. As this pattern continues, competitive individuals have an increasingly difficult time even knowing they have warm, sensitive feelings. This lack of awareness severely hampers their ability to form long-lasting, intimate relationships.

Competitive young people need patient help to risk opening themselves to their vulnerable emotions. Their personal vulnerability frightens these teenagers terribly because of their fear of losing control. Losing control of their emotions is even more threatening to them than not being in control of what's going on around them.

Effective modeling of emotional expressions is one of the most effective ways to help competitive teenagers open themselves to their own tender emotions. Let your children see you cry. Be willing to express affection in front of them—to your spouse, your other children, your pets and your friends. Be sure to express ample affection and love directly to your competitive teenagers, and encourage them to do the same. Suggest ways for them to communicate from their hearts to others. Help them select cards, write notes, give hugs, do chores and put their special feelings into words. Many of their fears center in their expectations of humiliation if they expose their vulnerable emotions. Reassure them of their okayness and respond to them in ways that clearly show you accept and value them.

Competitive young people guard against experiencing tender emotions, especially their own. Help them gain an awareness of how they feel; then encourage them to communicate their feelings to others. Learning to accept and share this tender part of their personality helps them grow toward wholeness.

11. Encourage your teenagers to develop a greater capacity to give to others. These adolescents perceive giving as taking something away from themselves. Their competitive orientation causes them to grasp all the power, attention, glory and acclaim they can for themselves. Typically, giving places attention on the gift's recipient. However, competitive young people handle their tension by giving in a manner that focuses more attention on their generosity or self-sacrifice.

Fear and personal insecurity normally motivate this kind of selfishness.

Help your teenagers by addressing the fears blocking their capacity to give. This task is difficult because these young people are usually unaware of their insecurities. Often they don't know why they resist giving. They only know they don't like to give. Giving makes them angry or uncomfortable even when they think about it. Talk freely with your competitive adolescents about the positive feelings you experience when you give to others. Let your teenagers know how good it feels to give to them. Be honest about any resistance you sometimes feel so your teenagers can identify with those feelings too. You'll have much more credibility with your children when you're honest and open about your negative and positive feelings.

Arrange situations in which your young competitors can give more easily. Go shopping with them and split the cost of gifts, especially those purchased for relatives. Give them numerous gift suggestions, and make a fun outing of your shopping, offering them plenty of reinforcing personal contact. Suggest they do extra chores to help those they care for. This physical act of giving allows these teenagers to get involved in the actual process of putting others first. Participate with them in a mission activity. Offer to help them take an active role in food drives, toy-collection campaigns and work projects that minister to the needy. Suggest mutually sponsoring a child in a famine-ridden country.

Competitive teenagers need your help to overcome their resistance to giving to others. The scriptural principles of dying to one's self and giving to others are difficult for these young people to embrace. Your assistance in this growth area can effectively impact their social and spiritual development.

12. Help these young people learn to accept God's grace and others' caring. Since competitive teenagers rely so heavily on their own competence, they struggle intensely with the concept of grace. Like power-oriented adolescents, these young people find it easier to rely on their own strength than accept God's grace. A merited reward is easier to understand and receive than unmerited favor. "What did I do to deserve that?" "I wonder why God would do this for me? The church is probably setting me up to go to the mission field." To accept God's grace means to rely on him. It means to trust in a superior love and caring. It means depending on a consistency, believing God will never let you down. All these concepts are difficult for competitive young people to accept.

Sometimes it helps to point out to these teenagers that they rely on God's grace without knowing it. Their bodies continually fight off infection, bacteria and other microbes attempting to invade their bodies. Their parents and other responsible adults care for their personal needs. Their national, state and local governments adequately provide for and protect them.

In addition, young people experience gifts of love, caring and forgiveness from one another. Work with them to understand that being served and receiving others' forgiveness provide growth opportunities rather than challenges to their pride.

You're now more familiar with competitive teenagers and can identify them more easily in your home. You must work with these young people to moderate the intensity of their competitive defenses and support them if they need help beyond your expertise.

CHAPTER THREE

The Aggressive Personality

For some teenagers, power isn't as important as aggression. Aggressive adolescents develop an effective and impressive way of relating to others. Sometimes they threaten and openly attack. Other times they're covert or subtle, but their intention is still the same. Their primary goal is to position themselves against others. They feel most comfortable when they actively oppose their peers and adults. They feel most threatened when others expect cooperation and closeness. They want interpersonal distance, which they accomplish by being aggressive and threatening to those around them.

Most aggressive teenagers use hostility as their primary defense and don't relate well to others. On the surface, these adolescents don't want close friendships. People are useful to them only when they can be pushed against. They feel their best when they're punitive toward others. While competitive teenagers try to demean and put others down, aggressive adolescents genuinely seek to intimidate others or cause them pain and psychological injury. They highly prize their aggressive tendencies.

Aggression is easy to identify in young people unless it's well-controlled and moderated. Effects of aggressive behavior are usually dramatic and memorable. Adults often express their aggression through stern, critical leadership such as a Marine drill instructor's. But during adolescence, few acceptable opportunities exist for expressing this personality type. During junior high and high school aggressiveness is intolerable both to other teenagers and the adults involved. Aggressive adolescents find it difficult to express their personality dynamics in appropriate, acceptable and constructive ways.

Aggressive adolescents make a statement to others. Essentially, they say: "I've been so wounded in life I can no longer trust or tolerate relationships with others. Therefore, I'll threaten everyone by showing them how aggressive and fearful I am. When anyone gets close to me, I'll hurt them back in return for the pain I've felt."

► *Development of the Aggressive Personality*

Although aggression is an issue for every adolescent, these teenagers have a difficult time controlling and moderating their aggressive impulses. Unlike power-oriented and competitive young people who attempt to control and dominate others, aggressive teenagers actively work to push others away. They learn to use their aggression as a defense to maintain a safe distance from others. A variety of dynamics in young people's lives influences their development of this particular defensive orientation.

1. Hurt during childhood. All adolescents have been hurt during their childhood. Aggressive teenagers, however, have been injured significantly enough to warrant developing hostilities toward others. Most aggressive teenagers have had psychologically painful experiences early in life. Some have been abused sexually, physically or emotionally. Others suffer from physical or emotional neglect. These teenagers have experienced other people as dangerous sources of pain. They've determined that their best approach to others is to keep them at a safe distance. And their most effective mechanism for accomplishing this task is presenting themselves as threatening and hostile so others will retreat.

God created us to need and enjoy contact with one another. His motivation for making Eve for Adam is in Genesis: "The Lord God said, 'It is not good for the man to be alone. I will make a helper suitable for him' " (Genesis 2:18). Each of the other defensive reactions in this book enables teenagers to make contact with others. Each personality type can find ways to overcome interpersonal anxieties in order to build and maintain relationships. Even though excessive use of the other seven defensive styles can eventually destroy relationships, their primary purpose is to protect teenagers from anxiety when they enter a threatening situation. Only the aggressive personality type is designed to actually push people away.

2. Aggression reinforces itself each time it works. Whenever aggression pushes others away, the teenagers' anxiety levels are reduced. Their security and comfort are enhanced as their anxiety levels go down. Thus, aggression succeeds; it accomplishes its purpose. And like the rest of us, aggressive adolescents continue to use what works for them.

3. Aggressive parents or other adults. Some aggressive adolescents learn their defensive operations from their parents or other adults. Sometimes children grow up in homes, neighborhoods or certain subcultures in which aggression is not only modeled by adults, but admired and praised. "Aggressiveness is the way to get what you want." From this perspective most interpersonal interactions are seen as aggressive encounters in which the most aggressive wins.

Criminal and gang subcultures are typically aggressive by nature. Aggression and intimidation rule. Young people from these subcultures use what they've learned in other settings too. When these adolescents enter a new group, they continue their attempt to lead with intimidation and toughness. They're similar to the "macho man," except their aggression is more overt. They openly display their bravado that says: "I'm tougher and meaner than you. Don't mess with me, or you'll get hurt."

All children try to emulate their parents, believing that in doing so, they'll please their parents. Unconsciously, aggressive adolescents also anticipate their adult role models will be proud of them and accept them as a result of their aggressive behavior.

4. Aggression is often misinterpreted as strength or power. Subtle expressions of aggression can effectively get people to "back off" without appearing conspicuously hostile or sadistic. Teenagers who behave this way usually gain a great amount of respect from their peers. Only when others get to know the individuals on a more personal level do they recognize their aggressiveness for what it is.

Aggressive boys often attract girls because of their "strength." Girls soon find out that this strength quickly turns into aggression when they get too close. If the aggressiveness is masked well enough, a young woman may not discover the truth until after an ill-fated wedding.

5. Reinforcement of certain forms of aggressive behavior. Sarcasm and quick comebacks are signs of being "cool" and "having it all together." In moderation, these behaviors work well. They win respect and elevate individuals within the adolescent pecking order. However, when used as the primary way of interacting with others, aggressive young people severely limit their meaningful relationships. Other teenagers withdraw respect and interest as they recognize the aggressive adolescents' cloaked intimidation and become fearful.

6. Adults' attention and praise. Some teenagers can mask their aggressiveness well enough to draw adults' attention and praise. They emerge as church youth group leaders or church board youth advisers. They win unsuspecting adults' admiration through their superspiritual feats. They rigidly hold to an approved lists of dos and don'ts. They have daily quiet times and avidly quote Bible verses. They express whatever is said and done in spiritual language. Within the Christian community these young people become excessively righteous and judgmental of others' sins. They view all of life through spiritual lenses.

This personality type's aggressiveness is seen in the rigid judgmental attitude expressed toward others. Some direct their guilt-provoking moralizations primarily toward their peers. Others aggressively criticize the adult community. Unlike competitive teenagers whose criticisms are meant to put others down, aggressive adolescents don't compete. They just want to make others feel pain. They actually want to intimidate or hurt others.

When you suspect your child of displaying inappropriate

aggression, examine these developmental issues. If you find several that fit, your suspicions are probably correct. We can't list all the possible reasons to explain an adolescent's aggressive personality. We can, however, offer common dynamics of the aggressive personality and list ways to parent these young people.

► Healthy Forms of the Aggressive Personality

The aggressive personality style is essentially antisocial. Therefore, one could argue that there are no healthy forms of this defense. If aggression and hostility are essentially unhealthy or sinful, how can expressions of this personality style ever be constructive? Aggression within teenagers indicates a problem in the young people's social adaptations. However, teenagers' abilities to moderate and control their aggression indicate other personality strengths. With God's help and a supportive community, all of us can control our negative or destructive impulses. This control strengthens all who attain it—even aggressive teenagers. Following are examples of how some adolescents moderately express their aggressiveness.

The Pious. As we discuss relatively healthy expressions of the aggressive personality, remember none of these has a particularly positive impact, either on the individual or on others in relationship to them. Piety, for example, is an important virtue. Pious people have great reverence for God and are deeply devoted to worshiping the divine. Unfortunately, "pious" may also describe individuals who are conspicuously religious and self-conscious about their virtue. In these cases, piety is only one step away from hypocrisy.

Wanda is quite a contrast to her brother Steve, who's three years older than she. (We'll meet him later in this chapter.) Wanda watched her brother go through difficulties at home, church and school. She observed her parents' reactions to his declining grades, poor choices for friends and periodic confrontations with the police. She witnessed vicious verbal battles between her father and brother. She not only saw the pain he experienced in his life of rejection, withdrawal and revenge, she felt the damage caused by his rage and hurtful behavior.

When Wanda was 7 and 8 years old, her brother sexually molested her on numerous occasions. Her rage was mixed with guilt because she enjoyed some of the stimulation. Her feelings' intensity threatened her so much that she repressed her memories and emotions associated with these experiences. Now, as an adolescent, she doesn't recall what happened. She doesn't realize why thinking of her brother makes her so anxious. Nor does she comprehend the psychological basis for her extreme piety.

Wanda saw commitment to God and a righteous life as the only way to be certain she'd never experience what she saw her brother go through. Her rigid, life-consuming religiosity also helped protect her from experiencing any sexual feelings normal for a girl her age. During junior high Wanda made a firm commitment to Christ. She'd been a Christian for several years, but as a seventh-grader she decided to dedicate her life to being absolutely obedient to God. She read her Bible regularly, attended church and Sunday school weekly and sought to apply what she read and heard to her life in every situation. Her religious commitment served as a protective wall. While presenting herself to others as the image of true spiritual devotion, this commitment guarded her both from her brother's threat and her own sexual impulses.

Wanda is now 16 years old. Her earlier pain has caused her to defend herself against all relationships. She trusts no one. Her brother, who she respected and looked up to, hurt her so deeply she unconsciously decided never to be close to anyone again. Her commitment to God represents a much safer relationship for her because she never has to confront God physically. In addition, she relates to God in an environment that she controls. Wanda finds people far more difficult to predict and control than her image of God.

Wanda's aggressive stance has obvious problems. She hurts and alienates others because of the pain she's received from and observed in her brother. But she's sought a constructive path for expressing her aggression. Her own devotion is certainly commendable, even with our deeper understanding of its basis. And her desire to manipulate her peers into an increasing spiritual commitment does have a positive thrust, though it's largely ineffective.

The Drill Instructor. In his church youth group Max is another blessing with numerous blemishes. In many ways he appears similar to Cynthia the "dictator," the power-oriented personality we discussed in Chapter 1. But their similarity ends not too far below the surface. To Cynthia, the issues are power and dominance; Max's purposes are aggression and the ability to hurt or threaten others. Let's examine how Max became the teenager he is today.

Max grew up in an extremely regimented home. His parents love him but don't express their love. Max has a sister four years older than he. She's bright, assertive and self-sufficient. All her life she's been gregarious, but also hesitant to express warmth or affection. During elementary and junior high school, she actively played sports, both in the neighborhood and at school. She's always been tough competition for Max. With only average intelligence and less-than-average physical coordination, Max has never been on an academic or athletic par with his older sister. Plus, her minimal expressions of affection have made him think she doesn't love him.

Both of Max's parents have compounded his problems. His dad is a career Marine who recently retired from active duty. Max's father personifies the image of the most rigid and authoritarian branch of the military service. Everything is "spit-and-polish." He controls virtually every activity in the house. Standards are high. He demands that his family meet his expectations immediately and consistently. Punishments are swift and severe.

Dad is even less emotionally responsive than Max's sister. He demonstrates his love for Max through providing financial security, a well-ordered home and strong parental authority. When asked about his father's love for him, Max responds, "Yeah, I know my dad loves me, but I sure don't feel it."

His mother expresses her love for Max with more emotion. She hugs and kisses him and tells him how she feels about him. Max feels that his mother loves him, but in a curious way his knowledge of her feelings diminishes her love's value. Her love is easy; it's always there. Therefore, his unconscious logic says her love can't be too valuable if it's so readily available. The difficulty of attaining his dad's and sister's love assures him that their love must have greater value.

When Max was in junior high, his parents had serious marital problems. They argued and fought, screaming at each other in front of the children. Max hated it. He feared they'd divorce, and he didn't know what would happen to him. His sister was no source of comfort; her comments offered no support. "Oh, all parents fight. That's the way it is. Don't be silly." He felt there was no one he could turn to for encouragement or understanding. He resented his parents for shaking his world and not being there when he needed their reassurance.

Max's anger at both of his parents and his sister continued to deepen. Somehow he needed to express these bitter feelings. Since his home was too threatening for such venting, his peers at school and church became his targets. He masked his anger to make it look like power or control, but his intensity and the self-righteousness in his stern, demanding attitude revealed the aggression beneath his control. Max is the one who demands quiet and cooperation from other young people when it's time to listen. Max is the one who volunteers to enforce "lights out" at the winter retreat. And of course, it's Max who would volunteer to monitor and report others' regularity in their daily devotions, if he could only figure out a way to do so.

Max has been deeply hurt and discouraged by the insecurity of his father's and sister's love for him. He feels rage in what he perceives as rejection; he also feels guilty about that anger. So he expresses it in a masked form (aggressive controlling) that unconsciously threatens, demeans and hurts others. Depending on how Max feels about himself, he can sometimes fulfill his "drill instructor" role in a relatively non-destructive manner. At times his aggression is well-hidden, but no mask can alter the aggression within him.

► Unhealthy Forms of the Aggressive Personality

We've already suggested that the aggressive personality is at its core an unhealthy adaptation to life and its stresses. This personality style presents an antagonistic front, contrary to our basic need for intimate contact. God created humans to draw naturally toward one another; aggression pushes people away. Less healthy aggressive teenagers are easy to identify because they leave such a negative impact on the people around them. In this section we'll examine three adolescent expressions of the unhealthy aggressive personality.

The Bully. We can compare the "bully" to both the dictator and the drill instructor. All three forms of social interaction involve exerting powerful influence on others' actions. The dictator seeks to control others through power and influence. Like the drill instructor, the bully stays in charge with intimidation and threat. But the bully's actions are even more overt and intense. Remember, aggressive teenagers want to hurt, or at least threaten to hurt, others.

Brad illustrates many personal and social dynamics of the aggressive adolescent. By age 13, Brad had experienced more pain than many adults. Four years after his birth, Brad's parents divorced. He lived with his mother and saw his father infrequently. During elementary school his mother invited nine different men to live with them. She married none of them, and most of those relationships lasted only a few months. She became pregnant several times and ended all but one pregnancy with abortions. Brad's little sister was born when he was 8 years old. He was expected to babysit his sister every weekday after school and during the evenings on most weekends. He was also given most of the household tasks as chores.

Brad's mother was so immature she could attend to no one but herself. And the men she lived with had no interest in being a father to Brad. He was an unhappy boy. He found little in his life to make it worthwhile. His unhappiness turned into anger. He became sullen, withdrawn and sometimes openly belligerent and aggressive at school. He'd never been popular with the other children or his teachers. Now he was gaining a reputation as a troublemaker. His downhill slide was gaining momentum, and there were no capable or concerned adults to stop or even slow his plunge.

Brad became discouraged. He knew he wasn't wanted at home. Although he used to have hope, he now knew he didn't belong at school or with the neighborhood kids either. He felt comfortable only when he was alone or with a certain small group of boys who struggled to alienate themselves from everyone else. He discovered that his own pain subsided when he hurt others. Brad pushed other kids around, brazenly cut into lunch lines and dared anyone to do anything about it; threatened to beat kids up if they didn't let him use their bikes; and forced kids to give him money for snacks and drugs. Almost all his social behavior was aggressive in some form.

By the time Brad reached early adolescence, he'd experienced the world as a hurtful place to live in. He felt people didn't care about anyone but themselves. He believed everyone would take advantage of him unless he could prevent it, and he learned he was on his own. He'd already experienced getting close to someone as a dangerous thing to do. And he responded to his inner pain and experiences by adopting an aggressive orientation toward others.

This aggression accomplished three tasks. First, it provided a release for the anger building in him throughout his childhood. Second, seeing himself as a pain initiator caused him not to feel so victimized by life. And third, this aggressive behavior backed most people away, allowing him to keep others at a safe distance. In this way he protected himself from further potential harm. Accomplishing these tasks provided continual reinforcement for his aggressive behavior. At the insistence of school personnel and the county probation department, Brad finally entered counseling. Unfortunately, without parental or other support, it's doubtful much progress can be accomplished.

The Judge. Remember Wanda, the "pious" teenager we met earlier in this chapter? Wanda's piety reinforced her feelings of okayness. She buried her painful, guilt-provoking memories beneath an exaggerated focus on God. She was aggressive in her efforts to help her friends become more spiritually devoted, but her efforts' intensity put others down and alienated them.

The "judge" is much more aggressive than the pious adolescent. There's no doubt about judgment when it comes from this type of teenager. This young person not only makes a judgment, he or she also passes sentence on others!

Phyllis is a college freshman. She's from a loving home where both parents are involved with their children. Both parents are Christians, and she's learned to live her life according to scriptural principles. Family activities have been adequately emphasized. Even annual vacations and special occasions have been family-centered. Phyllis grew up knowing she was loved and valued; so where did her problems develop? How did she adopt her aggressive interpersonal attitude if she had such a positive childhood family experience?

Her mother is a fearful, neurotic person. From an unhealthy, unstable family, Phyllis' mother carries personality scars, expressed in her negative view of the world. Becoming a Christian helped her forgive her parents for their lack of loving. Her faith also helped her release her past and live more fully in the present. But she can't (or won't) shake her fears about the future, and she's passed these fears along to her daughter.

"You can't be too careful, honey."

"Don't believe what people tell you. They're not being completely honest. They probably want something from you."

"Be especially careful around boys, dear. Most of them only want sex, and they'll tell you anything to get it."

She's drilled these and many other precautions into Phyllis since her early childhood. As Phyllis grew older, her mother had less control. With less control, her mom's insecurity and fears increased. Consequently, the intensity and frequency of her warnings about life's dangers also increased.

Had things gone well for Phyllis in her relationships with friends, she might have been okay. However, that wasn't the case. Every time Phyllis fought with a friend, her mother dwelled on it as further evidence of how disappointing and unfulfilling relationships are. Each spat or disagreement was another indication people should be shunned or at least kept at a safe distance. Phyllis took these experiences as ongoing proof that her mother was right.

Through early and mid-adolescence Phyllis became increasingly angry at her peers when they failed to do as she wished. When their actions hurt her, she became more indignant and accusing. The more she responded as a judge, the more her relationships deteriorated. She became increasingly judgmental of her friends' wrongdoings. She was verbal and confrontive. She took pride in her honesty and courage to tell others exactly what she thought. "You may not like what I say, but you'll always know what I think." She built a reputation for utilizing her honesty to inflict pain on others.

Her self-righteous attitude promoted her boldness. Her

defense worked tragically well. No one wanted to tangle with her. At the first sign of problems, her friends quickly backed away. Few were willing to confront her about her tendency to alienate so many friends. And when anyone did confront her, she used her notorious, airtight defense. First, she passed judgment. "You're being unloving (a lousy friend, unchristian, an uncaring person)." Then she delivered the sentence. "I'm not going to talk to you anymore." "You're no longer welcome at our church youth group." "With your bad attitude, you won't head any committees this year." "Since you haven't done any work this semester, you're off the leadership committee."

Phyllis goes way beyond Wanda in cruelty. Her goal is to hurt others by judging them "bad" and then making them suffer for their "sins." She enlists unsuspecting friends to help carry out her sentences by gossiping and turning them against one another. Those who trespass against her are likely to be banished from her "kingdom" or suffer another equally severe punishment.

Phyllis' self-esteem can't rest on being well-liked and accepted. Rather, it depends on how efficiently she can hurt others through her judgments and severe punishments. Since she's a Christian, much of her defensive behavior is filled with judgmental thinking and morality. She believes this religious aspect adds even more credibility to what she does. Unhappily, the way she uses scripture and morality discourages, hurts and distances her Christian and non-Christian friends. There's no ministry of reconciliation or healing in her actions.

The Sadist. Steve is 19 years old. (He's "pious" Wanda's older brother.) Throughout his life Steve has enjoyed inflicting pain on animals and people. In early elementary school he spent hours devising ways to torture bugs. As he moved through grade school, he began torturing neighborhood pets and any other animals he found. He'd sadistically stick pins through goldfish, drown cats, set dogs on fire and wound animals with his BB gun. He experienced excitement watching them struggle and suffer. Sometimes he was remorseful when an animal died, but this feeling never lasted long. His need for renewed arousal drove him to devise more creative ways to inflict pain on animals.

Steve also included people among his victims. Usually the pain he inflicted on humans was emotional rather than physical. He delighted in playing practical jokes on his friends. The problem with most of Steve's practical jokes was that they left the victims open to embarrassment and ridicule. These experiences were quite different from laughing with a friend. His victims experienced cruel mocking and relentless public exposure of their weaknesses, awkwardness or vulnerability.

As Steve entered junior high, he inflicted physical abuse and emotional cruelty on those around him. He fought with smaller kids and physically injured others. He tripped people on stairways, pushed them over while they rode their bicycles, threw rocks at them from behind bushes and even placed scorpions and tarantulas in his neighbors' mailboxes.

During sixth grade and junior high, Steve also began molesting his younger sister. At first, he coaxed her with candy, money and other small payoffs to let him do things to her. Soon the rewards ceased, and he began forcing his will. He threatened her with physical pain if she didn't submit to his wishes or if she told anyone what was happening. Their mutual fondling soon developed into his demands for intercourse and bizarre sexual practices. During one of these sexual sessions, his sister screamed with pain and bled. He became frightened and never molested her again.

Steve continued his aggressive sexual activity with other girls. He included elements of force, dominance, pain inducement, entrapment and total disregard for the girls' feelings. His arousal and pleasure seemed related to his use of violence or force as much as the experience's sexual nature. After he'd taken what he wanted from a girl, he always dumped her. This sadistic act with each girl was his final way of hurting and pushing her away, affording him the space he desired.

Steve fought viciously with his parents from his late elementary school years until he moved out of their house at age 18. He resented their rules. He couldn't tolerate their authority. So he struck out against them, seeking to intimidate, threaten and hurt them so much they'd back off. To some degree, his efforts paid off. They were unable to withstand the constant sting of his angry outbursts, the mocking or jeering when he succeeded in getting his way and the powerless feeling they experienced when he outmaneuvered them.

Steve's blatant aggression directed toward his parents was also expressed toward his teachers and other authority figures. Everyone received almost the same treatment. When individuals threatened to get close, Steve inflicted pain to make them withdraw. Nothing was ever his fault. Others were always to blame. Everything was externalized.

Steve is an angry young man who relates socially in only one way—aggressively. No one knows how this intense anger first developed. However, it's painfully clear that it has continued to intensify. Steve's aggression colors most every action, word and decision regarding his social relationships. His primary goal is to hurt others. When successful, he experiences brief relief from his own internal pain. And others instinctively back away, allowing him the wider comfort zone he desires.

► Effects of Aggressive Behavior on Others

Apprehension and fear are usually the first reactions people have when they confront an aggressive teenager. Even when aggression is moderated, people back off or take time to reflect on what's happening. These responses aren't surprising when we remember that the intention of aggression is to push people away. The protective mechanism of aggression presents itself in such a threatening manner that others retreat from the relationship. This distancing provides the adolescent with greater security and protection.

People resent being threatened. It's an affront to their dignity and security. They distrust the aggressive teenager's motives. And because of the threat or intimidation they experience, sometimes they distrust their own thinking and perceptions. An aggressive adolescent desires obedient submission as a response to his or her aggression. This type of submission is usually accompanied by the victims' resentment and desire to retaliate. A healthier form of the aggressive personality draws less severe negative reactions from others. Apprehension, fear, confusion and resentment are normally mild enough to allow others to maintain a relationship with this aggressive individual.

Another common response to aggressive behavior is guilt. This response normally occurs when confronted by a "pious" teenager. This aggressive youth flaunts his or her righteousness and morality, causing others to doubt their devotion, spirituality or okayness. This show of religious fervor is designed to stimulate inadequacy and self-depreciation in others.

The "drill instructor" often draws resentful compliance from others. People succumb to his or her pressure or the threat of some aggressive attack if they don't submit. In certain situations such as a football game, this approach is useful. In most social circumstances, however, other interpersonal responses are preferred.

An extreme form of aggressive social behavior is always destructive. The levels of fear, resentment and guilt that victims of an aggressive adolescent experience can become damaging. The "bully" can create deep fear in other teenagers that causes them to give up possessions, do something for the aggressor or in some other way comply to his or her demands. Humiliation, self-doubt and loss of self-respect often follow victims of this form of aggression.

The "judge" is a master at motivating others through guilt. His or her condemnations and punishing actions draw rage from individuals who experience this unjust treatment. Their guilt and self-effacement turn into rebellious reactions to the judgment expressed by this aggressive teenager.

The "sadist" operates socially by threatening physical or psychological harm. This is the most destructive and overtly aggressive form of the aggressive personality type. This young person feels best when he or she hurts others. The healthiest responses to sadistic behavior are fear and strong distrust, which lead the victims to withdrawal. Passivity, self-doubt and compliance to the sadist only bring further pain.

As you evaluate the effect an aggressive teenager has on others, remember this personality type is usually destructive to some degree. Other family members need protection from this type of young person. Adult intervention is not only appropriate, but sometimes necessary to minimize the negative effects of an aggressive adolescent.

► Guidelines for Parenting Aggressive Adolescents

Aggressive teenagers are among the most difficult young people to parent. Their defensive reactions, style of relating socially and ways of handling conflicts and interpersonal disagreements make living with them extremely difficult. Often they create turmoil, emotional pain and disruption in their families.

Offering love to aggressive teenagers who strike back in anger causes us to retreat because this rejection is painful. As a parent of aggressive adolescents, you need a strong support system. Spouses need to talk with each other and reinforce mutual efforts. Single-parenting this kind of teenager is exceptionally difficult. Whether you're single or co-parenting, you need the support of friends and relatives. You need to share your pain and parenting goals with your support system. Seek out other parents who're experiencing or have experienced similar parenting trials. Mutually supportive relationships are usually more successful than one-way support systems; but take advantage of what's available.

This book's purpose isn't to provide discipline guidelines or behavior control, but to help you understand and meet your teenagers' needs. This section includes specific ways you can help your aggressive adolescents develop healthier and more adaptive personality orientations.

1. Work to understand the origins and meanings of the aggressive behaviors expressed by your teenagers. Aggressive behavior is essentially unhealthy in most situations. When aggression is a young person's predominant behavior pattern, there's some underlying, serious cause. All people begin their lives wanting acceptance; all individuals initially desire warm, tender contact with others. A severe trauma early in life or a history of painful interpersonal relationships are the usual causes for developing aggressive interpersonal orientations. This social orientation suggests that these young people have given up hope for loving, positive relationships. They've succumbed to a lifestyle that keeps others at a safe distance. "If

I can push everyone far enough away, I can at least prevent further pain for myself." To aggressive adolescents, loneliness seems a better option than risking more pain.

As you recognize these tendencies and struggles in your aggressive teenagers, you're better prepared to respond to these difficult young people in ways that can help them heal. You can see and respond to their pain and fear instead of their aggression. These young people must learn to control their anger. Your primary thrust as a parent, however, should be to bring love and healing to your adolescents' injuries. Look for patterns in their anger. When do they usually explode? Which types of people do they push away? Look for clues to help you understand what they're saying through their actions.

2. Help your teenagers build a more positive self-concept. One characteristic common to aggressive adolescents is negative or low self-concept. These young people are usually just as angry at themselves as they are at others. The anger they express toward others often has its origins in self-directed rage. These young people view themselves as incapable of having meaningful or happy relationships. They may briefly think something is wrong with them. However, because that thought is terribly painful, they may project their anger onto others, especially you. A central part of your helping is making healing contact with your aggressive teenagers' hurting self-concepts.

Aggressive behavior is designed to keep others at safe emotional distances. Therefore, your aggressive teenagers may rebuff your efforts to understand and nourish their self-esteem. Your task as a parent is to keep trying. You need to be stronger and more tenacious than they. Take inventory of the things you respect and enjoy about your teenagers. Focus on their good and lovable characteristics, and let them know that you see and appreciate these qualities.

"I like your neatness and ability to keep things organized."

"You have an amazing knack for getting things done on your own. You're so dependable that way."

"Your sense of humor never ceases to surprise me! Your timing's fantastic, and you see things with a little different slant that makes them seem so funny."

Focus on your young people rather than their actions. By helping your aggressive teenagers develop healthy, positive self-concepts, you prepare them for altering their interpersonal relationship patterns. This is often difficult and discouraging work, but you can positively impact your children this way.

3. Help your teenagers increase their capacity for receiving love. Aggressive adolescents push away people who try to get close to them. Their defenses subdue their anxiety, but keep them from receiving anything positive such as warmth and love. Because of their restricted capacity for receiving others' affection, they may invalidate any tender responses you offer them. This restriction intensifies their isolation and reinforces their belief that they can't gain from relationships. As long as they hold these perceptions, there's little chance these teenagers will alter their interpersonal responses. An important part of your parental task is to help your young people open themselves to accept the love you and others extend to them.

Try a variety of ways to offer love to your aggressive sons or daughters. Some open themselves to receive one type of expression while others respond better to other forms of loving. Try saying it aloud.

"I sure do love you."

"We have our hard times, but I want you to know that none of those experiences make me love you any less."

Many of these young people reject loving words, but do receive loving actions. Surprise them with a plate of freshly baked chocolate chip cookies. Prepare their favorite meal, offer to run an errand for them, do their chores for a day, double their allowance for a week without having them do anything to earn it or let them stay home from school one day just to have fun. Be creative. Think about what your children enjoy; then surprise them. Experiencing your warmth and caring threatens these young people, but these expressions of your affection may gradually increase their capacity to receive love and help them make other important personality changes.

4. Encourage these teenagers to express their love to others. Aggressive young people react to expressing love and affection to others similarly to receiving love from others. Both experiences leave them feeling vulnerable and out of control. They're too close to their own feelings and other people to feel comfortable. Their most frequent recourse is to push others away with their anger to protect their bruised feelings and emotional sensitivity. Learning they can express love toward others without experiencing drastically negative effects is a major step toward their personal growth.

As a parent of aggressive adolescents, use your family relationships to help these children develop their capacities for giving love. Birthdays, anniversaries, graduations, Christmas and other special events provide natural opportunities for these young people to practice giving to others. Encourage them to give gifts and offer different expressions of appreciation or thankfulness. Help them determine what they can do for others; then support them as they decide how they can help or give to friends, loved ones or others in need.

Encourage these aggressive adolescents to verbalize their feelings to others. This form of expressing love may be difficult for them. People often feel most vulnerable when they tell others they love them. Some do better by writing their feelings. Let them start the best way they can. It's important that these young people start expressing their love and affection to someone, rather than pushing everyone away.

5. Let your teenagers know that emotional pain is a normal aspect of loving relationships. Most aggressive teenagers develop this social orientation because they've experienced significant interpersonal pain in the past. Some of them come to the conclusion that other people aren't worth the effort or the risk. Others believe there's something dreadfully wrong that causes their peers not to like or be attracted to them. The result is the same.

To prevent personal anxiety, these aggressive teenagers offend others or push them away with their anger, brashness or crudeness. Some of these teenagers, especially those who have experienced painful separations during their early years (such as their parents' divorce or a loved one's death), believe they can't survive another painful ending to an important relationship. They think they'd be just as emotionally helpless as when they were young children.

Help your teenagers know that choosing to love someone always involves a risk of getting hurt. Let them know some of your own history of pain in important relationships. Use good judgment and tell them stories about your own painful incidents with family, friends, girlfriends, boyfriends and even previous spouses. Be sure to include some positive experiences you've had in these loving relationships. These adolescents need to know that taking the risk to love can be worth it. They need to realize that allowing selected others to be emotionally close can add a new, vital dimension to their life.

These young people also need to know they can survive and even grow from the pain they encounter in meaningful interpersonal relationships. They need assurance that everyone who takes the risk to love periodically gets hurt emotionally. They need to know that emotional pain is not only normal and survivable, but a stimulating growth experience for most everyone involved.

6. Help your teenagers learn how to forgive others. The ability to forgive is fundamental to loving. Without releasing our anger toward others, we can never move on in relationships with them. Unresolved anger usually turns into bitterness, a desire for revenge or an intention to retaliate. Aggressive teenagers lack the ability to easily resolve their anger. Instead of forgiving others for their wrongdoing, they punish them with their intense feelings and make them withdraw. Therefore, aggressive adolescents seldom experience the pleasures of feeling forgiven by others, forgiving themselves or forgiving others.

You're in a strategic position to help your aggressive young people learn the value of forgiving. Observe your teenagers' interactions at home. Daily encounters among family members provide perfect opportunities for practicing forgiveness. In teaching your young people how to forgive, remember that forgiving is a two-way process. If you want your teenagers to learn this art, you must actively forgive them. Let them hear forgiveness in your voice and see it in your actions. Resolve your anger—and your personal need to punish their behavior—in some way besides directing it toward your aggressive adolescents. Help them feel free from your anger. Tell them you forgive them. Give them tangible expressions of your forgiveness and model evidence of God's forgiveness.

When you see opportunities for your aggressive adolescents to forgive you or other family members, observe how they handle the situations. Let them know that forgiveness is appropriate under these circumstances. Ask your young people if they know how to forgive someone. Remember, forgiving doesn't come naturally; it has to be learned. Encourage them to ask questions. Remind them that forgiving requires making a conscious choice to let go of whatever they hold against the other person. Let them know they must express their forgiveness in both words and actions if it's to have its most powerful impact. Forgiveness is one of the most difficult interpersonal actions for aggressive teenagers to accomplish. As you enable them to give and receive forgiveness, you provide the basis for their movement away from aggression as a personality orientation.

7. Help your teenagers become more aware of the effects their behavior has on others. Many young people perceive themselves and their actions differently from the way other people see them. They may not realize that their facial expressions, gestures, posture and body movements express emotions they think are well-hidden. Their body language often expresses feelings they've unconsciously repressed. Many times they don't recognize that their actions might impact others. Aggressive adolescents often communicate their anger in subtle yet powerful ways, but continue to question why others back away from them.

"Why don't my friends like me very long?"

"I don't get it. I guess there's something about me that turns people off."

Your adolescents need your loving but honest feedback. Even though they may not always welcome your insights, these young people need you to let them know when you see them do things that may offend or alienate others. You may see a sneer when they see a grin. You might hear sarcasm when they hear good humor. Their joke may sound to you more like making fun of someone. Often the most loving thing you can do for your teenagers is to tell them the truth. Make sure that when you give this honest feedback, you proceed in a loving, gentle way. "Sue, I'm sure you know I don't want to hurt you, but there's something I think you're unaware of that I've seen you do with your friends." Be careful not to express your anger indirectly in the way you tell them. "Sue, I don't think you have any reason to be surprised when your friends stop liking you. Look at what you're doing!"

Aggressive teenagers need honest, caring feedback from the people who love them. They need your loving confrontation with the truth. When they've been made aware of what they're doing, they're better prepared to make constructive changes in the way they approach others.

8. Help your young people direct their energies into constructive avenues. Aggressive teenagers often have high energy levels. They're active, enthusiastic people who have a wide range of interests. They typically enjoy sports and other recreational activities that involve physical activity, surface-level communication and light interaction with others. Since it's always easier to give direction to a moving object, these adolescents' high energy levels provide an excellent opening when you seek to help. These teenagers are active and in motion, even though much of their energy comes from their anger. Realize you can help them direct much of this energy into constructive channels.

There are many ways to utilize these young people's energies to reach positive end results. Involve their help and participation whenever possible. Let them take leadership roles in planning family activities. Help them develop the resources for giving to others. Encourage them to participate in activities that help them experience love, warmth and caring.

Aggressive teenagers can use the energy that comes from their repressed anger to learn more positive ways of relating. When they complain about their younger sister's childish behavior, have them play with her more often so she'll learn from their more mature ways. When they argue about how chores are assigned at home, place them in charge of designing an improved system and then presenting it to the rest of the family members for their modification and approval. When they express judgmental attitudes about another's behavior, request they make a serious proposal of changes they want the other person to make. Their proposal can then be discussed with just the other family member involved or the entire family. The primary task is to direct these teenagers' negative energies into constructive actions that stimulate positive feelings about themselves, others and their world.

9. Help your teenagers use good self-control while developing their critical thinking skills. A vital aspect of healthy adolescent growth is the development of critical-thinking skills. Aside from the obvious physical and emotional changes occurring during adolescence, there are intellectual developments that dramatically alter how adolescents view themselves, others, their faith and their world. These changes in their thinking processes are also prerequisites to their maturation into adulthood. During adolescence young people begin enlarging their ability to think abstractly. They formulate their thoughts in an "If . . ., then . . ." pattern. They compare options and develop possible solutions to numerous situations.

Teenagers must develop critical-thinking skills to succeed in their identity formation. Early and mid-adolescents typically criticize their parents, church, police and other authority figures. Often they're also extremely critical of their peers and even themselves. Critical thinking allows them to push far enough away from the beliefs, values and attitudes they've grown up with to develop their own thoughts and perceptions. Then, during late adolescence they usually begin to gravitate back toward the values they were raised with.

As a parent of aggressive teenagers, you may find yourself in a particularly uncomfortable position with your children. Being pushed away and rejected creates pain, and you need to defend yourself against this intense upheaval. However, your children still need your love, affection and acceptance. Offering them closeness that leaves you vulnerable to their criticism is particularly difficult when your children are aggressive adolescents who naturally overuse their critical defenses. As mentioned earlier, it's extremely important for you to develop a good support system. You need encouragement, nourishment and an active exchange of ideas for parenting these young people.

You need to encourage your aggressive teenagers to think critically while teaching them to control their hostile impulses. You can benefit from recognizing God's plan for parents to be in authority at home. "Honor your father and your mother . . ." (Exodus 20:12). Therefore, you don't need your children's approval or confirmation of your position: God has already confirmed it. You do, however, need to recognize a corollary to this commandment. As a parent, you must acknowledge the value of your children as ". . . created . . . in his own image . . ." (Genesis 1:27). Use your authority in a way that encourages your teenagers' development toward positive, constructive expressions of their critical-thinking abilities. When your teenagers express critical thoughts, respond with acceptance.

"That's an interesting point. Tell me more about your thoughts."

"I've never looked at it that way. I like the way you come up with your own views."

Express neither agreement nor disagreement. These young people don't want your judgment as much as they want your acceptance.

As a parent, encourage your teenagers to develop their critical-thinking skills as a normal part of adolescence. Since most aggressive teenagers tend to exaggerate their use of criticism, help them develop positive, constructive expressions of this trait.

You now have a better understanding of aggressive behavior and why some teenagers adopt this orientation toward the world. You are better equipped to help your teenagers with this orientation.

These aggressive young people are difficult to help. Growth comes slowly and with great difficulty. Realize you are not the only tool God can use as he continues his creative and healing work. Surround yourself with others who care about you and your teenagers as you strive to support these young people.

CHAPTER FOUR

The Rebellious Personality

Rebellious adolescents have much in common with the aggressive teenagers discussed in the previous chapter. Closeness and intimacy threaten both personality types. These young people have suffered common experiences including histories of pain, embarrassment and humiliation. Both types of adolescents associate pain with any prolonged social contact or commitment to a personal relationship.

While aggressive personalities retaliate by inflicting pain on others, rebellious adolescents are less interested in revenge. They want only to push others away or withdraw from social experiences. These young people are usually resentful, bitter and distrustful. Hurt or deprived during their early childhood, many rebellious teenagers never received the parental care and love essential to their early personality development. Many had parents who divorced during the kids' pre-adolescence. Others' parents both worked or for some other reason spent little time with them.

Usually these young people have also made poor social adjustments with their peers. They lack personal confidence because of inadequate social-skills training. They respond to their peers in awkward, displeasing ways. These experiences lead them into additional rejection and social alienation.

Rebellious teenagers typically internalize these experiences, blaming themselves for being unacceptable and unlovable to others. They're angry at themselves for not being more talented, attractive, intelligent or athletic. They're also angry at others. They experience bitterness and resentment about the rejection and alienation they receive from parents, siblings, friends and other adults.

The goal of rebellious teenagers is to protect themselves from further pain and emotional trauma by distancing themselves from others. Bitterness, resentment and fear influence their behavior. These young people struggle with mixed reactions. Those experiencing excessive resentment and bitterness push others away, while others who feel hopeless and afraid merely withdraw from social experiences.

Another difference between rebellious teenagers and aggressive adolescents is that aggressive adolescents have no intention of getting close to others. They're open and determined about their commitment to keep others away. Rebellious young people, however, are unhappy and frustrated with their social alienation. They want to be loved and even admit they want good relationships. Nevertheless, they experience deep conflict. When they begin reaching closeness or intimacy with someone, they sabotage the relationship, destroying the very thing they say they want. They can't tolerate the possibility of belonging, being part of a relationship, being included or being loved because it may bring too much painful anxiety or threat. So they deny themselves (and the other person) an experience they desperately need. Their behavior says: "I'm hurt and angry. I don't fit in with the rest of you. I can't and won't trust other people again."

► *Development of the Rebellious Personality*

Rebellion is a normal aspect of adolescent behavior. An important part of a teenager's identity formation is pushing away from parents, teachers, church leaders and other adult authority figures. All young people need to see themselves as separate and different from their parents. They need to develop their own identities. This process usually involves rebellion of some intensity. Therefore, possessing rebellious tendencies doesn't necessarily place teenagers in this category. We describe teenagers as rebellious types when their rebellion permeates and dominates most of their social behavior and responses to others.

Rebellious teenagers have problems in two areas. First, they have difficulty controlling their aggression. Their reactions may include anger, bitterness, frustration and criticism. These young people also have serious problems with submission. Hopelessness, lack of power and dejection usually combine with their aggression to create these rebellious young people. Let's examine some factors that cause teenagers to develop a rebellious personality.

1. Significant pain. Rebellious young people usually experience significant pain, especially early in life. This emotional trauma normally occurs in a relationship, particularly one with parents. When children experience significant rejection or alienation during the first few years of their life, they sometimes give up trying to belong. The pain seems too great to risk again. In addition to this fear of pain, they become angry and direct their anger both outward, toward the rejecting person and inward, at themselves.

Also, unhappy experiences with their peers are not uncommon for these young people. When they experience this further rejection in childhood, life's early lessons are compounded and reality becomes unclear. "I guess people really are dangerous." "I certainly can't trust in any friendships."

2. Inadequate affection, love or attention during early childhood. Through divorce, both parents working or incompetent parenting, these children don't receive the parental contact essential for healthy psychological and social development. Alienation during these early years robs children of important social learning experiences. Plus, this deprivation provides a shaky foundation for developing their self-concept.

3. Rebellious, negative parents. Rebellious teenagers have learned some of their negative perceptions from their parents. Children have learned to distrust others. They questioned others' actions and were suspicious of their motives. Throughout their impressionable childhood these young people listened, observed and learned from those around them. Perhaps they experienced negative conversations at the dinner table. Maybe they overheard the telephone gossip between Mom and her friends. They might have listened to

Dad's constant complaining about his unreliable co-workers. All these experiences could have contributed to their negative attitudes. Some things they experienced severely damaged their ability to relate positively to other people. With no concept of the impact they made on their children, these parents taught cynical attitudes about relationships.

4. It works. Like all defensive orientations, rebellion becomes a learned social reaction because it works. Pushing others away and withdrawing are rebellions that reduce anxiety. When people get too close, these teenagers feel threatened and experience tension. Each time they react rebelliously, others respond. The rebellious teenagers reduce their anxiety level and increase the chances of reacting similarly in the future.

5. Other teenagers often value moderate rebellion. Refusing to "go along with the crowd" makes young people appear strong. Questioning and holding back give the impression that these teenagers are particularly thoughtful and deliberate. Withholding themselves from others makes these adolescents appear superior and aloof. Standoffish social actions reinforce the impression that these teenagers are different. Unconsciously, this mildly rebellious behavior reconfirms their belief that they're special and shouldn't get too close to or overly involved with others.

6. Hero status. Mild critical rebellion can attract other adolescents, while hiding a multitude of fears and insecurities. Daring to criticize the establishment or defying the peer group's expectations appears courageous and powerful. Acting "cool," in control, and daring promotes rebellious teenagers to hero status among their peers. These young people attract admiration and attention from other teenagers while simply defending against the inadequacies they believe are within them.

By understanding this personality's developmental aspects, you can better identify and help the rebellious teenagers you live with. Instead of reacting to their surface behavior, you can understand more fully and respond to their deeper needs expressed by their actions.

▶ Healthy Forms of the Rebellious Personality

Rebellion is not only healthy but necessary for effective identity formation during adolescence. Even when rebellion becomes the primary behavioral choice, it doesn't have to be destructive or vicious. When rebellion is neither rigid nor extreme, it can work constructively for teenagers. Adolescents can gain several positive interpersonal benefits from their successful use of this defensive orientation. To maintain a healthy form of this personality type, teenagers shouldn't use rebellion excessively or inappropriately.

Following are examples of relatively well-adjusted rebellious teenagers. Both find constructive ways to live out their social orientation.

The Individualist. The Robinsons came in for professional counseling with their two teenage daughters—Brenda, 14, and Glenda, 13. Both girls provide examples of healthy, adapted forms of the rebellious personality.

The girls' parents married after discovering the wife was pregnant with Brenda. Even though they were in their late teenage years, they loved each other and were determined to do what they believed God wanted. Abortion was out of the question, and the young mother couldn't tolerate the thought of another family adopting her baby. In spite of their good intentions, they soon discovered they weren't mature enough to assume such adult responsibilities.

After two-and-a-half years of marriage, their second daughter, Glenda, was born. Financial pressures increased, and the girls' father showed signs of strain. Increased frustration, growing intolerance and frequent displays of temper accompanied his increasing alcohol use and decreased church involvement. Finally, when the girls were 3 and 4 years old, he left his family to live with another woman.

After their parents' separation, the girls seldom saw or heard from their father. His visits were few, and he never acknowledged their birthdays or other special events. Their mother worked at a low-paying job, and a variety of friends and babysitters cared for the girls. There was little structure in their lives; their routine changed almost daily.

Mom was still working when they started receiving counseling. There was only enough money for the necessities. Life was rather mundane for the small family. Brenda and Glenda had each other, but little contact with their mother. Both girls were developing rebellious personality patterns, but both had maintained surprisingly healthy levels of social adjustment.

Brenda, the oldest, had already become quite an "individualist." She felt lost and rejected when her father left. She'd also experienced a drastic change when her mother was forced to work. Her anger and pain combined to make these events traumatic to her childhood. She felt lonely and empty. Though most of her caretakers were kind, life seemed unfriendly to her. Peer relationships never worked out well. Feelings of distance usually prevailed, and Brenda felt that few of her friends ever liked her.

Brenda's rebellious response was to withdraw, and hers was a strong withdrawal. She didn't push others away; instead she actually pushed herself to a safe distance where she felt protected from interpersonal pain. She emphasized her individuality. She joined no clubs. She never played team sports. And she successfully resisted temptations to conform to fads in fashion, speech, interest and activities.

Brenda's limited money shaped part of her individuality. Her dress consisted of only jeans and assorted tops. Popular fashions changed around her, but she still wore her jeans. Rock stars came and went on the popularity charts, but Brenda remained faithful to one musical group. She collected their albums, covered her bedroom walls with their posters, wore their T-shirts and displayed their buttons.

Everything Brenda did proclaimed her individuality. She wasn't militant about it, just consistent and assertive. She showed no interest in football, basketball, baseball or track; however, she did enjoy speech. And her speeches provided her with a constructive way to make strong proclamations about her beliefs and principles. Her speeches, interests and activities all seemed to shout the same message: "I'm different from all of you. I'm an individual!"

The Antagonist. Glenda's early life experience was much like that of her sister Brenda. She too lost contact with her father at an early age, and felt both confused and rejected when he left. She also experienced sadness, pain and anger about her mother's lengthy absences every day.

Glenda was more successful than Brenda, however, in developing peer relationships. She wasn't afraid to let friends get emotionally close to her. During elementary school she had several long-term friendships. At church she also developed several meaningful relationships.

Adults were the primary target of Glenda's anger, distrust and suspicion. Adults had caused her pain and confusion; they'd removed themselves from her. So she chose to differentiate between how she responded to adults and how she responded to other kids. Closeness with her peers proved safe and rewarding, but intimacy with adults was painful and frustrating.

Glenda became a hero among her friends. She didn't fear confronting adults she disagreed with. Nothing was sacred. School rules, dress standards, church behavior and family expectations were all targets for her verbal attacks. She wrote letters to the school board, met with the principal, spoke out during congregational meetings and argued endlessly with her mother. Virtually all her contacts with adults were antagonistic. She was consistently critical, always finding something wrong with what adults either said or did. If she could find no fault with their actions, then their motives were at fault.

Glenda continued to kindle her anger and bitterness about her father's departure and her mother's absence. She felt powerless to change the situation, so she redirected her antagonism to the whole adult community. This response kept all adults away from her. She unconsciously protected herself from being hurt again. If she could keep adults far enough away, she'd be safe.

► Unhealthy Forms of the Rebellious Personality

Some degree of rebellion can be a healthy part of adolescent development, and rebellion is an essential element in identity formation for most teenagers. The individualist and antagonist take rebellion beyond its normal function during adolescence. These styles represent a well-adjusted degree of rebellion, excessive enough to warrant the label "rebellious personality," but well enough adapted to be healthy. We'll now meet two teenagers whose rigidity and intensity make their rebellious responses clearly unhealthy.

The Complainer. John is 13 years old. He's the third of four children in an upper-middle-class family. They live in a good suburban community and attend a well-established, traditional church. John's family members are recognized achievers. His father is a successful executive in a national corporation. His mother is active on several church committees, is involved with two parent-teacher organizations and chairs a community fund-raising group. John's brother and two sisters are also high-achievers. They're usually "A" students. His brother and one sister are good athletes, and his other sister is active in student government. All kids are fully involved in their church's active youth group.

John differs from most rebels because he didn't suffer early-life rejection in his family or his most intimate relationships. His family is reasonably close, warm and mutually supportive. His parents encourage each of their children to pursue activities they're most interested in and talented at. John hasn't found a lasting interest in much of anything, nor has he developed any particular abilities. He's average; and average can be a miserable state when one lives among exceptional achievers.

When John began preschool, it was soon obvious he didn't fit in, nor was he comfortable with the other children. He was never an outcast, and he never experienced actual rejection. But he never felt his peers accepted him either. He felt the same at church. In reality, most everyone accepted John, but they didn't include him or seek his involvement in what they were doing.

The one enduring social characteristic that describes John

in any group is his complaining. He whines. He's gained the nickname "Wimp," which certainly doesn't give his ego a big boost! The origins of his whining and complaining are difficult to trace. His parents say his complaining began during preschool and worsened throughout his childhood and early adolescence. Our best understanding of John's behavior indicates that during his early years he saw himself as inferior to everyone else in his family. His negative self-perception led him to feel insecure in this family of achievers. This feeling was accentuated when he entered preschool and again found himself performing less adequately than his peers. His self-doubts deepened, and his self-rejection intensified as he progressed through elementary school into junior high.

John's self-image as inadequate became well-entrenched, and he gave up trying to better himself. He's angry, frustrated and feels hopeless about his situation. Complaining is his only outlet. When things don't go his way, he whines. His low self-esteem doesn't allow him to express himself in a more direct fashion. He has only enough inner strength to release his bitterness through complaining. His behavior accurately expresses his personality's weakness.

John's complaining also accomplishes his rebellious defense another way. He soon becomes unbearable for most adults and peers. People avoid him. At the first sound of his complaining, people withdraw. His defense works. As others withdraw, his anxiety level is reduced. He withdraws into his own weakness and pushes others away with his obnoxious behavior. Of course, John then complains because no one wants to be his friend.

When asked, John says that he wants friends. He also admits he wants adults' approval. But he takes no responsibility for his negative interpersonal relationships. John's behavior illustrates the typical internal conflict of rebellious adolescents: They want relationships, but closeness creates such strong anxiety that they sabotage the specific goal they wish to attain.

The Delinquent. Charlotte's life provides a clear, unmistakable example of unhealthy adolescent rebellion. When referred to counseling, Charlotte was 16 years old, living in a group home as a ward of the court. Her parents never married and lived together only a few months after her birth. She lived with her mother and two older sisters in a series of small apartments. She attended several elementary schools, but was truant almost as often as she was in class. She had average intelligence but could read at only third-grade level when she was a high school sophomore. Her writing and grammar skills also fell far below expectations for her grade level. School made her feel uncomfortable and inadequate. With no parental support and limited teacher involvement, Charlotte's learning disabilities were never diagnosed. She falsely learned through her school failures that she was dumb. Discouraged and bitter, she felt forced to compete in an environment in which she knew only failure.

Charlotte received little attention from her mother. She was raised primarily by her sisters and grandmother. During elementary school, neighborhood boys sexually molested her on several occasions. But she never told anyone because the boys threatened to kill her if she did. These sexual encounters taught her she had something boys liked.

She also discovered she had something her girlfriends liked: the nerve to steal things for them. At first she stole candy bars, pop and toys. Later she took clothes, shoes, jewelry and radios at her friends' request. She kept a few items for herself, but most were "commissioned" by others or given as gifts.

Store employees caught her stealing several times during grade school. However, she usually charmed her way out of any serious consequences—until she was caught during sixth grade. At the end of a 10-minute chase through a shopping mall parking lot, Charlotte was apprehended with three bottles of perfume, two blouses, four swimsuits and a makeup kit. Charges were filed, and she was placed on probation. Three months later a similar incident occurred; and a week after that, she was caught stealing again. Because of her quickly lengthening police record and her lack of adequate adult supervision, she remained in juvenile hall four months. She was made a ward of the court and placed in a foster home where she stayed two weeks. The foster parents returned her to juvenile hall because they couldn't prevent her stealing food, clothing, jewelry and money from their home.

Her second stay in juvenile hall lasted eight months. The court attempted another foster home placement. This one lasted almost a year. Everything appeared to progress satisfactorily until authorities discovered her foster father was regularly having sexual intercourse with her. She was transferred back to juvenile hall once more and finally moved into the group home where she lived when she initiated counseling.

Charlotte had little in her life to feel good about. The only security she'd experienced came from her own efforts, and those moments of apparent safety passed quickly. She honestly believed only those adults who wanted something from her would try to get close to her. Charlotte learned how to "out-use" them. She believed her friends would remain only as long as she could provide something for them. Therefore, the items she stole, the drugs she procured and the sex she provided were the commodities she traded for acceptance.

Charlotte had a brief church experience when she was 13 years old. At a friend's invitation, she attended a small church and its youth group for a few months. But she felt so different from the other church kids that she stopped attending. Unhappily, her church attendance became another experience in failure, alienation and perceived rejection.

Charlotte began learning her rebellious lifestyle at an early age. Her adaptation to her world resulted in an obviously unhealthy and unacceptable social orientation. To Charlotte, people became objects to outwit, out-use or avoid. Social rules were for bending, interpreting or breaking for her benefit. The basis of her morality narrowed to, "Whatever helps me get by is good, and whatever blocks me from get-ting what I want is bad." Her delinquency succeeded in keeping people at a safe emotional distance. And she effec-tively alienated others by repeatedly offending them with her behavior.

► Effects of Rebellious Behavior on Others

A rebellious adolescent has an overwhelmingly negative effect on others. This teenager directs much of his or her underlying hostility and bitterness toward adults. Peers are attractive as long as there's mutual need-fulfillment. As soon as the rebellious adolescent fails to gain from this exchange, the apparent closeness ends. This individual deliberately sabotages any relationship when closeness or intimacy re-sults in anxiety.

When confronted with rebellion, most people are con-fused and upset. "Why's he doing that?" "I can't believe she's acting this way." "It's hard to guess what's coming next!" This type of teenager exposes underlying bitterness and distrust of others through his or her rebellious behavior. Unsure what these actions mean, others feel vulnerable and uncertain. Their spontaneous reaction is to back off, allow-ing sufficient space to think through the situation objectively.

As people continue experiencing rebellious behavior, they typically react with irritation or anger. Helping adults even-tually lose their patience. They become angry when their best efforts to nurture and support are degraded or rebuffed. They withdraw from the rebellious teenager to protect themselves from the pain of personal rejection.

A rebellious teenager commonly provokes others' rejec-tion. Healthy, loving people don't enjoy a bitter, distrustful or sullen individual. This type of teenager has a toxic effect on others. When the toxicity level reaches a certain point, others have to protect themselves by rejecting the young person or pushing him or her away. (Try to identify a rebel-lious personality in your family. Do you withdraw or push him or her away from you? If so, you recognize the need to protect yourself from this type of teenager.)

Another common response to a rebellious adolescent is to

retaliate by putting him or her down. Competitive individuals usually use this natural defense to protect themselves from the pain or inadequacy a rebellious adolescent fosters. Some adults exert their position, dominance or greater strength in a way that enhances their perceived superiority over this personality type.

Most reactions to a rebellious teenager's behavior are punitive. Angry shouting, criticism or rejection are effective punishment for this type of individual. But by the time many adults begin working with one of these adolescents, their natural reactions to the young person's rebellious behavior have temporarily sabotaged their ability to help.

Overt rebellion pushes others into anger or withdrawal. These negative reactions confirm a rebellious adolescent's distrust of others. This lack of trust increases underlying bitterness and resentment toward others so the individual can defend himself or herself by rebelling again. In this negative cycle, this personality type keeps creating and re-creating his or her own world of alienation and isolation.

Rebellious adolescents remove themselves from relationships in numerous ways. "Individualists" find security by using constructive avenues for being alone and self-reliant. "Antagonists" keep others at a distance through continually criticizing those who might attempt intimacy. "Complainers" repulse others with constant whining about life and its unfairness. "Delinquents" actively push others away through illegal, antisocial behavior. Each of these teenagers uses a type of rebellion for protection from feeling-related anxiety and a need for interpersonal relationships.

▶ Guidelines for Parenting Rebellious Adolescents

Like the aggressive young people in Chapter 3, rebellious teenagers create significant challenges for parents. Their behavior is not only trying, but wearing. They often cause family disruptions and make it difficult to resolve conflicts. Remember to rely on your spouse, other family members, friends and other teenagers' parents for support. A good support system provides a "listening ear" for your frustrations and problems. It also offers opportunities for others' input on how to work with these difficult young people. Since rebellious teenagers are among the most difficult adolescents to parent, this section is designed to offer help and support in understanding and responding to your young people's needs.

1. Work to understand the meaning of your rebellious teenagers' behavior. Rebellious teenagers act out their feelings in ways that get adults to react strongly. Their rebellious behavior often threatens and angers authority figures. Then, acting directly from their emotions, adults respond defensively or angrily in ways that intensify unhealthy dynamics in these adolescents. Instead of reacting to your emotional impulses, try to understand and respond effectively to what your rebellious teenagers' behavior actually says.

Rebellious teenagers have usually experienced emotional pain, especially in early-life relationships. As with the aggressive adolescents we met in the previous chapter, these young people are angry. They lack the self-confidence aggressive young people have; therefore, they handle their anger through either active or passive rebellion. Usually, they pull away from others, but it's an angry pulling away. Rebellious behavior essentially says: "I've been hurt and disillusioned in relationships. Therefore, I'll withdraw and discourage you from trying to help me."

Your parenting task is to listen effectively for the needs your rebellious teenagers' behavior expresses, rather than react to their behavior itself. Try to hear their pain, anger and fears. Listen for their understanding of what they feel has happened to them.

2. Help these young people find release from their past emotional injuries. Teenagers usually select rebellion as a personality orientation because of emotional pain in earlier childhood. Many of these young people have been rejected, left (as in a divorce or parental separation) or abused. Others have had extremely difficult or unsuccessful experiences trying to fit in with neighborhood children and kids at school. They've learned that interaction brings pain and disappointment. They've also lost confidence in themselves as individuals who can succeed in relating to others.

You can help your rebellious teenagers work through and

let go of their past emotional hurts. Encourage them to gradually talk out their feelings. Listen quietly to them when they tell you about their painful experiences. Many of these experiences probably include you since parents are usually the most important people to young children. Listening and encouraging them to talk requires great patience and selfless love on your part. This doesn't mean you should allow your adolescents to verbally abuse you. Let them know when their conversations become destructive. Encourage them to talk honestly about their pain without condemning others.

Rebellious teenagers need to release their emotional pain and anger before they can successfully grow into healthy adults. You can be your children's best source of love and care by listening patiently.

3. Help your teenagers become less angry with themselves. By experiencing your acceptance and support, aggressive teenagers can let go of their personal guilt and anger and accept themselves as they are. Associated with aggressive adolescents' pain are anger and guilt. These young people are angry at others for not providing love and fulfilling relationships for them. And they're angry at themselves because they're unable to interact with and attract others. Being angry both at others and themselves, they feel deep guilt. They perceive themselves as too weak, ineffective and unattractive to succeed in their relationships. Judging themselves as failures, they rebelliously set themselves apart from others out of fear, anger and guilt.

Your love and acceptance are probably your rebellious teenagers' most effective healing sources. Their self-doubts and tendencies to demean themselves express their deep needs to be cared for. Be sure to include them in special activities. Provide one-to-one activities that offer communication and relationship-building opportunities. Invite them to help you with projects. Assure them of your appreciation while you work together. Involving your children in your life is one of the most effective ways of saying: "I value and highly respect you. You're worthy of my love and relationship." As they experience your respect, they can begin to value themselves more highly.

Reassure your rebellious adolescents that all of us have

made serious mistakes in our pasts. Get personal. Tell your sons and daughters about some errors and failures lurking in your childhood or adolescence. Help them understand they can have major problems in their past and present and still have successful, constructive adult lives. Teach them about redemption and the life-changing power God extends to everyone. Guide them in learning how to obtain his grace through confession, repentance, obedience and seeking ways to extend love toward others.

Rebellious adolescents desperately need to let go of their anger and guilt. Your support and acceptance can have a major impact in releasing your children from these crippling forces.

4. Help your teenagers reduce their distrust levels by being a trustworthy parent. Teach your adolescents how to recognize others they can trust. One of rebellious adolescents' hallmark responses is a strong distrust of others. Because these young people suspect others' motives, their lack of trust pours out in angry sarcasm or demeaning attacks on others' values, intents and actions. By considering others unworthy of their interaction or involvement, these adolescents effectively distance themselves from others and protect themselves from the possibility of further pain. The intensity of their distrust is particularly dangerous because it may result in a lifelong perceptual bias. Distrust can become an ingrained part of their attitude that severely restricts their desire and ability to form meaningful relationships.

The quality of your relationships with your sons or daughters can either help or hinder their ability to trust others. One of the greatest gifts you can give your teenagers is your own trustworthiness.

Are you dependable?

Do you follow through on your promises?

How consistent are you?

Do your actions fit with what you say?

Can your children accurately predict how you'll respond to various situations?

Can they trust you to keep their confidences?

Do they believe you'll act on what you think is best for them?

Your answers to these questions indicate your trustworthiness from your children's point of view.

When critical thinking reaches the extreme proportions common to rebellious teenagers, it may lead to intense distrust of almost everyone. You can help your children accept others' failures and imperfections. Point out the presence of good and bad in everyone, including themselves. Tell them that choosing to trust or distrust isn't an all-or-none proposition. Everyone can be trusted for some things, but a few people can't be trusted for almost anything. Encourage balance in their perceptions of others.

Rebellious teenagers tend to distrust others. Encourage them to risk trusting others to help them remove one major block impairing their ability and freedom to form fulfilling, intimate relationships.

5. Help your young people realize that emotional pain is a normal part of relationships. Rebellion is designed as a defense to protect adolescents from emotional pain and a sense of weakness. Often these threatening feelings arise from unhappy and injurious interpersonal relationships. Many young people don't realize that everyone experiences occasional emotional pain while building relationships. Romantic, work and family relationships and friendships are all vulnerable to the imperfections of the people involved.

Just knowing "I'm not the only one," can relieve someone who's hurting. Gently reassure your daughter when her boyfriend doesn't ask her out. Comfort your son when his girlfriend breaks off their relationship. As part of their consolation, help them realize painful experiences are a normal part of adolescence. Reassure them that just because others have had similar experiences, you're not saying their pain shouldn't be taken seriously. Recognize their hurt and let them talk with you about their feelings. Also let them know that almost everyone survives this experience. They need to know that life won't always look as hopeless and depressing as it does now. These young people need to know they aren't flawed because they've experienced painful relationships. You can play a major role in offering them reassurance.

6. Realize that some rebellious adolescents don't want to experience expressions of love. These young people have been injured seriously enough to convince them that they can gain nothing from loving relationships. They've assumed the position of not wanting love. Remember, this isn't an all-or-none trait; not all rebellious teenagers are extreme in their personality dynamics. While some adamantly reject love, others are just mildly resistant. Nevertheless, all rebellious adolescents distrust and avoid loving relationships to some degree.

When you force your expressions of love on rebellious teenagers, they may react in one of two ways. First, they may become aggressive. They may act out their anger toward you or displace their aggression onto a safer individual such as a younger brother or sister. Second, these young people may respond by internalizing their anger toward you. With this response they become more self-depreciating and guilt-ridden because of their inability to accept or respond to love. When you don't recognize or respect the resistance your adolescents put up against you, you force love on them. Excessive hugging, kissing, gift-giving, doing activities with them, making them be with you and excessive verbal expressions of "I love you" are all ways to unwisely force love on your rebellious young people.

It's a difficult struggle when your children reject your love. When your love is effectively blocked, you aren't sure what else you can do. Some helpful suggestions:

• Respect your teenagers' defenses. When they need space away from you, allow it.

• Don't try to overpower them. If they resist your hugs and kisses, don't force them. Listen when they say: "Please stop. I'm uncomfortable with this."

• Offer your need for love and allow them freedom to respond when they're comfortable. Comments such as "I need a hug. Do you have one to spare?" allow your child to say "Yes," "No" or "Not right now." If they see they can control and limit these expressions of affection, they may be more willing to risk. Remember, responding to another's request is a powerful way for both you and your children to communicate love.

• Be flexible. When your teenagers reject one expression of love, try another. When they push away a verbal "I love you," try doing something special for them. Fill up their car's gas tank; buy them freshly cut flowers or a plant for their room; surprise them by doing their chores; or leave an "I'm thinking of you today" card on their breakfast plate. Be creative. Brainstorm new ideas with your spouse or friends. When one thing doesn't work, that's okay. Try something else.

Rebellious teenagers characteristically reject your attempts to express love, so you need flexibility and creativity to communicate your love in ways your children can accept. This patient process helps your adolescents gradually open themselves to accept love and affirmation from other important people in their lives.

7. Focus on accepting your rebellious teenagers rather than approving their behavior. Acceptance focuses on people while approval focuses on their behavior. These teenagers desperately need affirmation that they're accepted. They're filled with self-doubts about their inadequacies. Approval of their performances in statements such as "You did a great job," "I'm amazed at how well you handle those situations" and "I'm extremely pleased with how well you're doing" have little influence in helping rebellious teenagers improve their self-concepts. It's okay to offer those kinds of affirmations, but realize that these responses to their behavior have a less positive impact than responses that focus on the individual. Some examples of appropriate accepting responses:

"Shirley, I'm not sure you realize how much I enjoy having you in our family."

"Bill, your sense of humor adds so much to our family. I like having you here."

"There's so much that I like about you, Mark. I'm going to miss you when you go to school."

Each of these responses focuses more on teenagers' personal characteristics than on their behavior.

Rebellious teenagers may easily argue that their performances or skills aren't that good. They're quick to refute your positive appraisal of their competencies. It's much harder for them to counter statements that you enjoy or value them. Your messages of personal acceptance gradually accumulate within them and powerfully impact their capacity to develop a higher level of self-esteem.

8. Encourage your teenagers to express more tenderness toward others. Expressing soft, tender emotions frightens rebellious young people because they feel vulnerable, and vulnerability is exactly what their rebellious orientation is designed to protect against. Because these teenagers lack self-confidence, they withdraw from close contact with others. Experiencing warm feelings threatens these young people two ways. First, it frightens them by bringing them closer to others in an affectionate, caring manner. Second, rebellious young people usually misinterpret their warm, soft feelings to mean they have personal weakness and incompetency. This misunderstanding verifies their self-condemning beliefs.

Expressing tenderness toward others is extremely threatening for rebellious young people; however, it's important for them to develop this capacity. Adult relationships will require their commitment and intimacy with important others. Dealing effectively with tenderness and warmth is an important part of developing their relationship skills. Help your adolescents increase their capacity to deal with tender feelings. Model expressions of these feelings in your own actions and words, both toward your family members and friends. Let your young people see how these emotions can benefit you and those you express them to. Point out situations in which risking your own vulnerability by expressing your feelings was rewarded with another's love.

Rebellious young people often find it less threatening to expose their vulnerability to younger children than peers or adults. Encourage their tenderness toward younger brothers and sisters. Arrange for them to play with younger cousins, nieces, nephews and your friends' small children. When sensitive emotions and tender interpersonal issues are presented on television or in the movies, elicit your teenagers' responses to that material. See if they can express their feelings while watching those situations. Get them to talk about how they might have felt if they were in similar circumstances.

Rebellious teenagers resist warm, tender situations with others. Help them adjust to their emotional vulnerability as they prepare for healthy adult relationships.

9. Help your teenagers involve themselves in assisting other people. Rebellious teenagers often avoid helping others because they lack self-confidence and fear emotional vulnerability. Offering help places people at risk; their help may be rejected or ridiculed. Others may see their offers of assistance as inappropriate or weird. These young people are acutely aware of the personal risks they take when offering help. Their lack of confidence actually sabotages their capacity to help others. Offering assistance presupposes belief that one's personal skills and values are potentially beneficial to others. Low self-esteem characteristically causes these teenagers to disclaim any positive belief in themselves and underestimate their abilities to help others.

Helping has a central value in Christ's teachings. It also plays a significant role in developing healthy interpersonal relationships. Therefore, as part of teenagers' spiritual and psychological growth, these young people need to develop their ability to help others. You can assist your rebellious young people by maximizing their chances for success in helping ventures. Structure situations that don't seem dangerous or threatening to them. Since helping younger children is usually less threatening than working with their peers or adults, request their help with younger brothers and sisters. They might set up and run birthday parties. Perhaps they could teach their younger siblings how to play games or work with them to develop new skills such as bike-riding. They could also help them with their homework or babysit.

As your rebellious teenagers gradually gain confidence in their ability to give, encourage them to offer help to their peers or adults. Suggest ways likely to produce success and good feelings so they'll gain confidence in themselves and their abilities. Building their capacity to help can provide another way for these young people to develop healthier relationships with others.

10. Help these young people develop greater trust in their own strengths. One difference between rebellious and aggressive teenagers is rebellious teenagers' lack of confidence in their inner strengths. Initially, they withdraw from others and internalize their anger. They often blame themselves for their perceived inadequacies and then live with long-term guilt. This insecurity in their abilities then produces even more anger and guilt within them.

You can be a vital support as rebellious adolescents seek to build confidence in their inner strengths. Think about tasks they can do that will expand their confidence in their abilities. Are there specific chores that would help them see themselves as responsible people? Place them in charge of meal preparation one or two nights a week. Offer them responsibility for washing and waxing the cars or changing the oil. Perhaps they could do laundry or help with ironing. Suggest they take care of the rose bushes and fruit trees or make them responsible for the house plants. Give your teenagers tasks that require developing special abilities and learning new skills. These tasks should have more meaning than taking out the trash or picking up in their room.

Encourage your teenagers to tackle new tasks. Start with easier ones to maximize their chances for success. Help your young people develop self-concepts that say, "I can learn to do important, valuable things."

Interpersonal relationships also present opportunities for your rebellious adolescents to gain confidence in their strengths. Developing social skills, gaining ease in relating to a wide variety of people and assuming leadership responsibilities encourage them to believe in their strengths. Rebellious teenagers need to find good reasons to trust their worth, value and strengths. You can help your teenagers prove to themselves that they do possess trustworthy inner strengths.

11. Encourage your adolescents toward more positive expressions of their critical-thinking skills. Without the ability to think critically, teenagers can't adequately evaluate ideas, values, thoughts and attitudes. They must learn to analyze their thoughts to develop their own faith, beliefs, attitudes, value systems, preferences, likes and dislikes. Failure to develop critical-thinking skills produces adults incapable of thinking for themselves. Rather, they align themselves with people they respect and copy or assimilate their beliefs, attitudes and values.

Rebellious teenagers often exercise their critical-thinking skills in only negative or destructive ways. They may criticize their parents, teachers, police, Sunday school teachers, pastors and even their friends. They also become exceedingly self-critical. Help your rebellious young people exercise their critical-thinking skills to think positively as well as negatively. Help your teenagers sort the good from the bad when discussing a person's character. When they criticize a teacher's action, ask them if they see anything positive in what their teacher did. As they speak critically about a friend, ask if they can balance their view with positive observations. When they make disparaging remarks about themselves, encourage them to list their beneficial characteristics also.

Rebellious teenagers can be excessively negative in exercising their critical-thinking skills. You can help them temper their views with positive evaluations. This guidance can help your rebellious adolescents reach a healthier balance in the way they view the world and themselves.

12. Work patiently with these teenagers as they try to grow. Remember, individuals grow at different paces. You can't demand your adolescents to change their behavior when you think they should. They are their own persons; and though they sometimes need encouragement, reminders or prodding, you must respect their internal clock. Self-concepts, defense mechanisms, emotional blocks, repressed pain and anger, fears, insecurities, and their ways of perceiving reality affect the rate at which they accomplish certain changes. It's helpful for us to remember the patience that God and others—even our own parents—had with us!

You express great respect and love for your teenagers when you're patient with them. This caring, valuing message can have an additional positive impact on your adolescents as they continue maturing.

Though rebellious teenagers are difficult to help, you now have tools that can help you work successfully with them as they move toward growth and healing.

CHAPTER FIVE

The Self-Demeaning Personality

Self-demeaning young people are the least likely to be noticed as having problems because of their ability to retreat into the background. They purposefully avoid attention and are quick to shun responsibility. Perhaps their strongest psychological feature is their lack of belief in themselves. They see themselves as inferior and incompetent. These adolescents are the most submissive of all personality types.

Self-demeaning adolescents are the opposite of the power-oriented young people discussed in Chapter 1. Instead of finding security in strength, these teenagers emphasize their weaknesses. Leadership positions and vulnerability to others' expectations create strong anxiety in these young people. They don't possess the aggressiveness of competitive, aggressive or rebellious teenagers. They withdraw passively, rather than angrily withhold themselves like rebellious teenagers. When they do become angry or frustrated, they direct their hostility and negative feelings toward themselves. They don't possess the energy or self-confidence required to effectively express anger toward others.

Demeaning oneself is one of the most direct forms of self-protection against excessive anxiety from interpersonal contact. These young people actually hide from others. They conceal themselves from possible failure while they hide from others' expectations, judgments and rejections. Success even brings increased anxiety; these young people fear that when they publicly succeed, people will expect more—increasing their chances for future failure. Self-demeaning behavior essentially says, "I want you to believe I'm a weak, incompetent person so you'll expect nothing from me."

► Development of the Self-Demeaning Personality

Most adolescents experience periods when they need increased quiet and privacy. During these times they spend hours in their bedrooms, listening to their stereos, drifting in fantasies. This withdrawal is common during early and mid-adolescence. It accompanies the task of identity formation that consumes so much of teenagers' psychological energy.

By itself, this behavior doesn't suggest a self-demeaning personality. When teenagers withdraw and express self-depreciating behavior over a long time period, however, we should be alert. If this behavior continues and then links itself to our teenagers' inadequate self-concepts, we must assume that our young people are developing self-demeaning personality patterns. Several causes commonly emerge in the personal histories of self-demeaning adolescents. Let's identify some important causes and understand how they contribute to this personality type's formation.

1. Lack of sufficient training at home. When parents are inadequate socially, mentally or otherwise, they have difficulty providing their children instruction and experience in the interpersonal skills required to live effective lives. Other parents consciously withhold their love, affection and important teachings because they resent their children.

Some young people are raised in homes where both parents work; others are raised by a single parent. In these busy families, managing a schedule plus numerous jobs, household tasks and social obligations leaves little time for effective parenting's demanding requirements. In these situations young people miss important training that leaves them inadequate in many social arenas. They may not know about or have much experience in building relationships. They may feel uncertain about communicating their feelings or accurately understanding their peers' behavior. These deficiencies typically lead to interpersonal awkwardness, social rejection and further belief in their own inadequacy.

2. Lack of adequate parental nurturing and encouragement. What happens during early childhood dramatically impacts young people's psychological development. Young children desperately need their parents' affection. Infants know they're loved when their parents hold them, talk to them and attend to their basic needs. When parents deprive their children of adequate love, children develop intense insecurity and strong self-doubts.

Negative or neglectful early-life experiences falsely teach young people they're neither valuable nor important enough to warrant others' interest. When young people have no personal support, they typically accept this devastating, false conclusion. These teenagers, then, continue performing actions that reflect their negative beliefs about themselves.

3. Criticism of their strengths. Most parents are well-equipped to love and care for young children. However, many parents reach their limits during adolescence when their children develop more personal strength and begin asserting themselves as individuals. Teenagers easily challenge insecure adults. Assertive adolescents threaten parents who question their own identities and sexuality. Young people who idealistically forecast their great successes intimidate parents struggling in their own careers. Other adults may believe any boasting is sinful and resent these young people for their bad taste and inappropriate behavior.

When parents, teachers and other adults struggle with their identity or resent teenagers' efforts toward maturation, they often criticize young people and discourage their independence. In many cases these adults project their anger on relatively defenseless young people. The adolescents then blame themselves for displeasing adults. By internalizing adults' anger, these young people chastise themselves for their pride. They also battle guilt that arises each time they experience personal strength, independence or other steps toward maturity.

4. Taking on excessive guilt. Some adolescents take on excessive guilt with little adult encouragement. This is particularly true of self-demeaning teenagers. These sensitive young people often misinterpret scripture and pulpit messages to mean that all positive thoughts about themselves and all positive actions on their own behalf are wrong. They mistake their personal recognition of maturity for pride. They view healthy self-concern as selfishness. These teenagers become their own most severe critics. They judge themselves harshly for personal confidence and strength, qualities essential for continued growth and maturity. Unfortunately, churches and church youth groups sometimes reinforce this self-punitive thinking, forgetting that we're all God's valuable creations.

5. Misinterpretation of passivity and withdrawal. During childhood and early adolescence, peers sometimes mistake passivity and withdrawal for strength. Self-demeaning young people's defenses work so well they can fool adults and even their closest friends. Consider how often women choose the "strong, silent type" of men, only to discover their masculine "dreams" are passive, insecure boys. Masks of quiet strength and superior "cool" effectively hide withdrawal and passive personalities. When friends reinforce these self-demeaning skills with fear and respect, teenagers will probably use these psychological defenses more and more.

6. Reinforcement. Teenagers who successfully learn to express self-demeaning defenses reinforce their self-depreciation. Their defense's effectiveness leads to a reduction in their anxiety level. Their coping methods lessen their fears and insecurity about interactions with others. Remember, these young people fully believe in their inadequacy. They're convinced that they are somehow insufficient and undeserving. They expect rejection, ridicule and negative judgment from other teenagers and adults. Therefore, when their fear and anxiety are reduced by these negative experiences, they seek to reinforce these feelings by seeking more of the same. After several years of this pattern, altering their behavior becomes difficult. To change, they must challenge the beliefs that they built their defenses on—they must begin to believe they are okay. This attitude change automatically creates more anxiety, which discourages growth.

As we live with our young people, it's important that we

increase our awareness of their personal histories. How have they become who they are today? Which forces impacted their personality development? Which experiences helped shape their behavior, thought and emotional patterns? Our awareness of their background and how they view it increases our understanding of their present behavior.

► Healthy Forms of the Self-Demeaning Personality

In our complex culture, avenues of social interaction vary. Opportunities are available for the healthy interaction of virtually all personality types. Demeaning oneself is certainly not a healthy dynamic at its core; however, the young people described in this chapter can find adaptive, constructive ways to interact with others. There's one crucial element—their interpersonal behavior patterns can't be excessively rigid or intense. They must develop the ability to moderate and adapt their interpersonal style to fit with different people in different social situations. Following are two case studies of self-demeaning teenagers who made healthy adjustments in their personality orientation.

The Modest. Jill is kind and considerate to everyone she knows. Adults especially enjoy her. From her teachers and Girl Scout leaders to her youth minister and her mother's friends—all adults find Jill respectful and considerate. Jill finds adults less threatening than her peers. She notices that most adults don't talk to her or other high school kids much; and when they do, they're usually satisfied with a smile and polite response. Then they leave her alone.

Jill's peers also like her, but they have a hard time getting to know her. Although self-consciousness is normal for most teenagers, Jill is extreme. Any attention goes beyond discomfort; it's actually unbearable. To avoid these unpleasant situations, Jill seeks anonymity. She operates as an average student, attempting to repel any attention, whether negative or complimentary.

Jill's personal history helps explain her modest behavior. When she was 4 years old, her father was killed in an industrial accident. Shortly after his death, Jill and her mother moved to another city to be close to relatives. Once they arrived and settled into the community, they joined the local church, and Jill was enrolled in violin lessons.

When Jill's mother was finally forced to work, she began expecting more of Jill. Her mother relied heavily on her for housework, cooking and other chores. Just before Jill's 11th birthday, her mother met a special man in their church and began considering remarriage. Jill's mother encouraged her to attend a few brief sessions with a professional therapist to help her adjust to the possible change in their family life. When Jill was 12, her mother did remarry and quit working outside the home. By this time Jill had so incorporated her mother's values, she altered her lifestyle very little, even though less was required of her.

Jill is now a high school junior and an excellent musician. She's continued her violin lessons and thoroughly enjoys playing her instrument alone at home. She struggles terribly with public performances. When she has to play at school concerts or during church programs, she panics. She's just as uncomfortable after her presentations as before and during them. Because she's so talented, everyone wants to congratulate her and express their appreciation. But the awkwardness and embarrassment she experiences from this extra attention are more than she can handle.

Nothing's wrong with Jill, except her excessive modesty. She's managing her life well, but why is she so modest and shy? When compliments are directed toward her, why does she respond with comments such as "No, not really; it was nothing," "Anybody could have done as well" or "It was God, not me"? Her self-consciousness goes beyond discomfort. And her discomfort's intensity doesn't appear to diminish.

Throughout her childhood Jill heard her mother stress modesty's value. She was disciplined not to be proud. Her mother also emphasized the importance of considering others before herself and giving God credit for all the good she accomplished. With her mother's emphasis on these modest values and extensive responsibilities, Jill learned to think her own needs and wants were unimportant. She also believed she was secondary to others. She felt most comfortable when she was last in line or when she got the smallest piece of cake. She continually struggled with guilt both before and after purchasing nice clothes for herself. Asking for something or being assertive was difficult for her. Modesty permeated every area of her life. Even though Jill is a self-demeaning teenager, she's essentially a psychologically healthy adolescent. She relates well to her peers and exceptionally well to adults.

The Servant. The youth leader had known Walter since he was 6 years old, when he first came to the church with his family. Now in the eighth grade, 13-year-old Walter has been in the junior high church youth group for two years. His personal history provides an interesting example of factors that can lead to the development of an adolescent self-demeaning personality pattern.

Until he was 6 years old, Walter's life seemed completely normal. He lived in a loving family atmosphere, the youngest of three children. Though small for his age, he adapted well during preschool and kindergarten. Other children liked him, and his teachers reported good progress in school.

Shortly after entering first grade, Walter complained of hip pains. His parents noticed a slight limp and took him to his pediatrician. Further consultations with an orthopedic surgeon revealed a congenital problem in the development of his right hip socket. During the next six years, Walter had four surgeries and spent 54 months in the hospital. During this important part of his childhood, his whole life was focused on his physical problem and its correction. Because of his traction, casts, braces and physical therapy, he was unable to attend school for months at a time; so he was tutored at home.

To fulfill his need for social contact, he depended on friends who came to visit him. His church youth group also supported him. Their periodic visits and special arrangements included Walter in as many activities as possible and helped him keep feeling that he was still part of the group. Fortunately, his family was loving and supportive. They did their best to attend to his needs without spoiling him.

During the months following his rehabilitation, Walter returned to his school, friendships and church youth group activities with full intensity. But the way he became rein-

volved was particularly interesting. At school he became a towel boy in the boys gym, helped his English teacher after school and served as the manager's helper for his school baseball team. His friends recognized him as an excellent person to ask for help with homework or other projects. Walter arrived early for every church youth meeting and helped set up chairs. He spent extra hours preparing papers, organizing handouts and helping his youth leader with anything else that was needed. He also remained after each event to help clean up. At home he faithfully completed his chores and sometimes volunteered to help his older brother and sister with theirs.

Walter made sure he was always involved and available to help, but he never took any leadership position or authority role. He declined every invitation to lead prayer, give announcements or organize activities. He seemed to avoid being noticed. He felt comfortable socially only when he helped or served others. Receiving from friends, relatives and family members without opportunity to reciprocate during his rehabilitation had made him uncomfortable. He had to be doing something for others. Yet his self-confidence wasn't developed to the point he could function well in any leadership capacity.

Walter's physical difficulties severely hampered his social development. By resisting the dependent type of contact he had from age 6 to 12, he became a servant to others' needs to allay his own feelings of uselessness. It was the one social role he felt comfortable and confident enough to fulfill. Walter had done a marvelous job of adapting to and recovering from a difficult life experience. His level of social involvement was remarkable, but it was also seriously limited. Walter would need encouragement and guidance to help him relate to others in more ways than just as their servant.

▶ Unhealthy Forms of the Self-Demeaning Personality

While most personality types strive to develop positive experiences to fulfill their needs, the self-demeaning personality strives to feel better by experiencing pain. This personality pattern is one of the most difficult to break because it thrives on negative feelings that normally deter behavior. Like the child who playfully places his finger on the stove to get his mother to notice him, these young people willingly stick their hands in the flame to receive a scream of attention. We'll look at three unhealthy patterns of self-demeaning behavior in this section.

The Recluse. At her mother's insistence, Shana initiated professional counseling when she was 19 years old. She was 5 feet 11 inches tall and weighed over 200 pounds. In her first session she said little. Angry at being forced into counseling, Shana used her silence as a weapon to preserve her dignity. To talk freely with the counselor would have meant losing the power struggle with her mother. Although this reaction is common for a teenager forced into counseling by parental pressure, there was something more involved in Shana's silence. Three times she told her therapist, "If I can't even talk with my mother, how can I talk with someone I don't know?" Something inside blocked her from releasing her thoughts and feelings to others. Something inside kept her from making contact with people who cared about her.

Therapy progressed slowly at first. Shana had difficulty developing trust in her counselor's care. Finally, the invitation to open up to her inner pain and turmoil in her counseling sessions' safe environment proved too much for her defenses. Gradually, mixed with many tears, her story emerged.

Until her sophomore year in high school, Shana enjoyed life. Her family provided adequate, though not outstanding, love and support for her and her younger brother. She was an avid athlete, playing soccer and softball on community teams since she was 6 years old. She went through school with her best girlfriend from early elementary to high school. She was a strong-"B" student and reasonably popular, both in her neighborhood and at school.

Shana's psychological development progressed well, and her future looked promising. Then in her sophomore year, everything seemed to go wrong. In a few months, her life crumbled. And during the past five years, she has unsuccessfully tried to pull herself back together. Let's examine the combination of losses, pressures and rejection that overwhelmed Shana. They're the same forces that seriously affect many teenagers.

First, Shana broke off her friendship with her best girlfriend. Inseparable for 11 years, both girls desperately wanted to date the same boy, and Shana lost.

Losing the boyfriend was the second event that contributed to Shana's devastating sophomore year. This young man and her girlfriend dated steadily until a few months before Shana initiated counseling. Thus, between the ages of 15 and 19, Shana was not only without a best girlfriend, but she had never experienced a positive relationship with a boy.

The third negative event of Shana's 10th-grade year came during a school volleyball practice. Diving to return a difficult ball before it hit the floor, Shana severely damaged her knee. Her injury forced her out of volleyball for the rest of the school and community league seasons. Since volleyball was her best sport, Shana's outstanding performances were her primary source of affirmation and ego support. Now they were gone for the rest of the year.

Shana's fourth major blow was also related to her knee injury. She was one of her school softball team's leading players. When she was injured, the coach removed her from her regular first-base position and allowed her to participate only as a designated hitter. The coach's decision was appropriate, but Shana viewed it as another rejection. She'd lost one more valuable source of affirmation for her personal value and identity.

During this pivotal school year Shana experienced her

fifth trauma. As Shana's schoolwork deteriorated while she struggled with everything happening in her life, her English teacher remained cold, demanding and emotionally aloof. Instead of expressing concern and finding out why Shana's work was declining, her teacher criticized her and openly shamed her in front of the class for not working up to her potential. That was a turning point for Shana. She gave up; she broke. Now she was in therapy, desperately trying to regain the developmental losses she had accumulated during the past five years.

At age 15 Shana gave up and withdrew from those around her. It wasn't a violent withdrawal such as the rebellious adolescent's. She merely retired into passive hopelessness and gave up on life. Her pain was too great. Too many of her supports had been knocked out from under her. Trying to succeed in athletics, academics and relationships had led to pain, rejection and failure. Shana became a recluse. She avoided all contact with people, unless absolutely necessary. She walked alone to and from school and spoke to as few people as possible while there. She did only minimal school-work, passing her classes with a "C" or "D." Shana even withdrew from her family, forcing them to initiate interaction if they hoped to converse with her.

Many times Shana had felt suicidal, but told no one she was in such danger. Her withdrawal's intensity and the depth of her hopelessness had become a pattern. Her interactions with others were self-destructive and self-demeaning. She felt she had no value. She chose to believe she could never succeed. Her negative self-image was the only way she could feel okay about not trying to succeed in any area of her life.

The Martyr. Beverly is a 16-year-old high school junior. Her behavior reminds us of Walter, the servant teenager in the previous section. Beverly also does things for other people. She, too, is helpful in her church youth group. She does the tasks most kids neglect. When volunteers are requested and few respond, Beverly is almost always available. Since she got her drivers license, she provides regular transportation for other youth group members to meetings and other activities. She runs errands, moves equipment and is generally available to do whatever needs to be done.

Beverly is similar to Walter in another way. She's comfort-able relating to her peers and adults only when she's help-ing or providing for someone. Her youth minister, who's known her six years, says Beverly has operated with this be-havior pattern since he's known her. Each year she assumes more responsibility in doing things for others.

There is one aspect of Beverly's behavior that differs from Walter's servant pattern. Even though Walter limits the way he relates to others, he enjoys serving them. Beverly, how-ever, resents her social position. She readily volunteers to do a task and then completes it with a self-righteous air: "I'm more willing than you to work hard. I always pick up where you fail. Therefore, I'm exceptional."

In much of Beverly's attitude toward others, there is im-plied anger mixed with her self-righteousness. Like most martyrs, Beverly is angry that others make demands upon her. Like most good martyrs, she doesn't accept any respon-sibility for choosing her role. She feels victimized, and in subtle ways projects her anger at those around her. She al-ways makes others pay in some manner for the work she chooses to do for them.

A look at Beverly's significant personal history explains why she might have developed into an adolescent martyr. Beverly was the eldest of three children. Her father was an alcoholic who became a binge drinker when Beverly was 4 years old. About five times a month, he'd drink every day until he passed out on the family-room couch. These binges would last up to three or four days. Other times he'd leave one evening for his favorite bar and not return until the end of his binge several days later. Many times he'd come home in a drunken stupor. Sometimes he was belligerent and an-gry, and other times remorseful and apologetic. But Bever-ly's mom always calmed him down and cleaned him up when necessary. Finally, Beverly's mother was forced to take a full-time office job because of her family's decreasing in-come and the increasing costs of her husband's addiction. In addition, she took a part-time waitressing job, which necessitated her working many evenings and weekends.

As the eldest daughter, Beverly was required to take over

many household duties such as cooking, doing laundry, ironing, and watching her younger brother and sister. Beverly was destined to become a martyr. Her mother was the perfect teacher, and her childhood home was the perfect breeding ground for developing a self-demeaning personality. Her mother spent many hours complaining about how hard she had to work, how unfair it was that her husband was an alcoholic and how she'd surely leave him if it weren't her "Christian duty" to care for him. "After all," she'd remind Beverly, "it's not every woman who could put up with what I do day after day."

By the time Beverly entered adolescence, she had mistakenly learned that her only value was meeting others' needs. She felt guilty when she received anything positive for herself. Although she was angry about not having her needs met, she felt she had no right to her own happiness or personal fulfillment. She avoided friendships with peers. Even though she attended all church youth meetings, she never found the time or opportunity to go to their socials. Her self-demeaning pattern became self-limiting and destructive, and she desperately needed professional help.

The Masochist. One of the most tragic forms of the self-demeaning orientation is the masochist. Teenagers who develop this pattern learn to associate pain and personal loss with pleasure. They usually have destructive personal histories. Leon's case history helps us see how this unhealthy personality pattern can develop.

Leon initiated professional therapy when he was 17 years old at the insistence of his physician. Within nine months of getting his drivers license, he had been involved in seven automobile accidents. Five were minor and never reported to either his insurance company or the police. In four of these minor accidents, Leon was driving the only moving car. In one instance he scraped a parked car while trying to parallel park. On another occasion he hit a tree while backing out of a friend's driveway. On two other occasions he hit parked cars, one while trying to enter a diagonal parking space and the other while driving down a residential street. His fifth minor accident took place in the school parking lot and resulted in crumpled bumpers on his and another student's car.

His two serious accidents occurred within the short span of three weeks. On both occasions he collided with cars that had come to a full stop in front of him. Mild injuries and several thousand dollars in car damages were sustained in both accidents. Leon rapidly gained the nickname "Crash" with his friends. He personified "an accident waiting to happen." Few of his friends' parents would allow their children to ride with him. And after his second serious accident Leon's physician advised his parents to take him to a professional therapist.

As counseling progressed, Leon's background and the reasons for his frequent accidents were revealed and more clearly understood by his therapist. Leon was the younger of two children. His sister was seven years older, and he was the unexpected, unwanted "surprise" that arrived when his parents were in their early 40s. Leon's father was gruff, stern, and sorely lacked communication and parenting skills. His responses to any misbehavior were yelling, cursing, hitting and any number of belittling putdowns. Raised in an abusive home, Leon's father never learned how to express or receive physical affection. Leon couldn't remember his father ever telling him he loved him or giving him a hug.

Leon's mother wasn't a big improvement. Her marriage to Leon's father was her third. During her childhood and in both of her earlier marriages, she'd been the victim of physical violence. She received financial support and companionship from her marriage, but didn't expect a positive or fulfilling relationship, especially with a man. She had thought she wanted to be a mother. But shortly after her daughter's arrival, she realized she resented this baby's intrusion in her life. Therefore, Leon's accidental conception and unwanted birth seven years later made her anger and rejection return. She resented the physical discomfort and pain associated with her pregnancy. And she immediately withdrew from Leon after his birth, punishing him with her rejection.

Leon's sister also resented him. Forced to assume much of his parenting and caretaking throughout his infancy and childhood, she became bossy, cruel and punitive toward him. She teased him incessantly and ridiculed him in front of her friends.

Leon's childhood was miserable. Tragically, his family taught him that he was unwanted, unlovable and inadequate. He felt he had no personal value and didn't belong in his home. During early childhood he expressed rage at his mistreatment. However, the physical and psychological pain of his family's cruel and abusive punishments taught him to internalize those strong emotions. He soon learned it was safer to blame and hate himself than express his anger toward anyone else.

Leon grew into adolescence with no confidence in himself as being socially acceptable. He had no self-esteem, and his bag of social skills and other resources for meeting life was empty. Desperate for attention, he had to gain some type of acknowledgment. Anything was better than nothing! So Leon picked up where his sister and parents left off. He learned to make fun of himself. He gained skill as the "straight man" who was always the butt of his own joke. He finally learned how to gain attention, and any type of attention felt like acceptance. He became a buffoon, a clown.

He began associating the pleasure of being noticed with the pain of being laughed at by others. At least being laughed at offered some form of attention. His search for acceptance became a continual reaching out for new ways to experience social derision and humiliation. His physical clumsiness, social awkwardness and even serious accidents became sources for his pain-pleasure connection. By the time he initiated therapy, Leon was a severely disturbed boy. His self-concept and way of interacting with others contained little that was healthy. Leon's rigid, intense masochism combined with limited support from his social environment had produced a guarded and doubtful picture for his future.

► *Effects of Self-Demeaning Behavior on Others*

At first glance it appears that self-demeaning behavior benefits only the young person exhibiting the behavior. Like all interpersonal actions, however, this type of behavior is directed at others and draws certain responses from them. The responses most commonly received correlate with the kinds of people the adolescent feels most comfortable with.

A self-demeaning teenager prefers people who reinforce self-depreciating feelings. As he or she assumes the role of clown or buffoon, others respond with laughter and demeaning responses. These reactions are particularly intense when others are convinced this adolescent is really inept, foolish, clumsy and inferior.

Initially, a self-demeaning young person elicits sympathy and caring from others who are concerned and want to help. But when others' responses bring closeness, warmth and intimacy, their positive, helpful efforts threaten the self-demeaning teenager to the point he or she pushes them away. Caring people are soon discouraged and give up trying to help. Their positive efforts give way to irritation and frustration. Repetitive self-depreciating acts eventually anger these people whose help has been thoroughly discouraged.

A self-demeaning teenager often gravitates toward young people who act arrogant and superior. He or she may choose to spend time with power-oriented and competitive young people because these teenagers naturally behave in ways that feel comfortable to the self-demeaning adolescent. These teenagers disapprove of, laugh at and put down others who appear inadequate and foolish. This type of mutually unhealthy relationship brings out the worst in both personalities.

A self-demeaning teenager also assumes undignified roles. He or she subjects himself or herself to others to be used in self-derogatory ways. Being used enhances a self-perception of worthlessness.

► *Guidelines for Parenting Self-Demeaning Adolescents*

Self-demeaning young people often experience significant

psychological pain, but most people don't realize these teenagers are hurting. Others not only don't recognize self-demeaning teenagers' pain, but are oblivious to their presence. The self-demeaning social orientation enables these teenagers to go through interpersonal situations virtually unnoticed. Even those who care for them often miss these adolescents' painful struggles. In this section we'll look at many ways you, as a parent, can help your self-demeaning teenagers.

1. Seek to understand the origins and meanings of your teenagers' behaviors. You're in a unique position to understand how your adolescents feel about themselves and how well they are doing with their lives. You gain your understanding not only from what your teenagers say, but even more from how they behave. You're more aware of your children's personal histories than any teacher, minister or counselor. As you observe your young people's behaviors, think about what's happened to them in the past. Notice behavior patterns that help you understand their present actions.

While some teenagers feel awkward receiving any kind of attention, others are only uncomfortable with positive attention. Many teenagers strive to help others, but teenagers with histories of physical abuse may seek to help in different ways from adolescents who were nurtured in their early childhood. Your teenage son's shy, withdrawn behavior around girls means something different from his shy, retiring behavior around everyone else. Observe your young people's actions carefully and then seek to understand their behavior's meaning in relation to their past.

2. Help your teenagers understand the meaning of their behavior. Understanding why we act as we do is often the first step toward making desired changes. Insight alone rarely makes us change our behavior, but it helps. Teenagers usually need guidance to understand their behavior's meaning. They're unaware of the reasons or motives underneath their actions. Their typical response to "Why did you do that?" is "I don't know." Even though this response may frustrate you, it's usually honest. Children consistently express their emotions through their behavior, while adults verbalize their feelings. Teenagers operate somewhere in between. Even though they discuss their feelings and thoughts more than younger children, they still function less consciously than adults.

With your teenagers, gently suggest possibilities about why they act as they do. Use extreme caution. Recognize that humans defend against self-awareness for a good reason—there are truths in us that would upset us if we suddenly became aware of them. So suggest the least-threatening possibilities first. Then, as your teenagers accept their inner feelings and motivations, gradually suggest more potentially threatening possibilities.

For example, your 17-year-old daughter may be shy and especially withdrawn around boys. She claims she has no idea why she avoids boys her age. Initially, you might suggest she lacks experience with her peers, especially boys, and therefore feels uncomfortable.

In later conversations you might point out that since she's never dated, she might be afraid no one will ask her out. She may be avoiding this possible "failure" by avoiding boys. If she accepts this possibility, you might imply that she could be scared of not knowing how to act if a boy asked her for a date.

At a still deeper level, you might help her recall a negative experience that may affect her behavior. Perhaps she was sexually molested by a relative or babysitter during early childhood. She may unconsciously fear that something similar might happen on a date. Only when she recognizes and accepts this possibility can you ask if she's afraid of not being able to control her sexual impulses or others'.

Helping your teenagers understand why they act as they do can help them gain a feeling of control of their behavior. This awareness helps them feel more comfortable with themselves and more secure about their development.

3. Help your teenagers correct their negative self-perceptions.

These young people characteristically have negative self-images. Their family, social and school histories have probably assured them they have little value. They mistakenly assume they're also unworthy of meaningful relationships. Their self-concepts focus on the negative aspects of their bodies, intellects, feelings and behavior. Some of these young people can see only their negative traits. When asked, they can't report good things about themselves.

These teenagers need positive feedback from people they trust. And contrary to popular opinion, your adolescents can develop trust in you as their parent. One way you can earn your teenagers' trust is by being honest in what you say. When you tell your negative thoughts and opinions to your teenagers, your children have more reason to trust you when you're positive. Develop a believable balance between your negative and positive observations. A 14-year-old girl told her counselor: "Of course my mother told me she thinks I'm attractive. How is she going to say I'm ugly? She's my mother!"

Build trust in your adolescents that you'll always tell them the truth. Remember, honesty can be kind and gentle or harsh and uncaring, depending on how you offer it. Parental love necessitates telling the truth in healing, uplifting ways. Telling your self-demeaning teenagers the truth can help them correct their unrealistic negative perceptions about themselves.

4. Listen to your teenagers and assist them in their efforts to resolve past injuries. Most self-demeaning teenagers have histories of significantly painful experiences or long-term hurtful relationships or events. These unhappy histories have taught these young people not to believe in themselves. To build positive self-concepts, teenagers must release and resolve their painful pasts. They can't accomplish these tasks alone. Even if you're centrally involved in some of their pain, there are past hurts in which you can help your teenagers release their pain and heal their injuries.

One of the most important ways you can help your self-demeaning adolescents is by encouraging them to discuss their feelings. Spend time with them. Arrange one-to-one opportunities conducive to discussing feelings. Go to dinner together. Take a walk, or work on a quiet task together. Have a regular Bible study time and pray with each other. There are many ways to help your young people begin talking with you about their pain.

When they do discuss some of these past hurts, listen and let them know you hear them. Give them verbal responses that indicate you understand. For example, your youngest daughter may complain: "You always listen to Karen first. She always gets her way." Acknowledge what she's said. Calmly repeat her thoughts back to her in your own words. "I can hear your concern about your oldest sister. It sounds like you feel we put Karen's needs and wants before yours." This reworded response allows adolescents to correct any of your misunderstandings before resolution can take place.

Help your young people realize that past experiences may affect their lives, but don't have to control them. Remind them that accepting God's grace can help release them from their pasts. They need to know how to forgive those who have hurt them. They need your support and care. Releasing hurts and emotional injuries from their past is necessary for adolescents' personal growth. You can play a major role in this part of your teenagers' psychological development.

5. Help your teenagers reduce their feelings of helplessness and hopelessness. Self-demeaning adolescents are convinced they're weak and incompetent. They feel inadequate to live life effectively. They believe they're unworthy of meaningful relationships. Remember, not all self-demeaning young people operate in the extremes of this personality orientation. While some experience severe incapacity, others demean themselves only when under stress.

Most self-demeaning teenagers feel helpless, and this helpless perception of themselves leads them to feel hopeless. Typically they don't believe they have the power or ability to improve their situations. They see others as in control. Since having personal control of themselves and their world is central to healthy adolescent development, self-demeaning teenagers are often depressed. If anything positive is to occur in these teenagers' lives, they believe it must come through someone else's effort.

Help your young people experience more control and power in their lives. Structure situations your teenagers can have success in. Encourage your children to try tasks that help them develop positive self-esteem. When your adolescents perceive themselves as competent young people who can grow, develop skills and accomplish important achievements, their feelings of helplessness will wane. As they experience success and observe their progress, their hopelessness will diminish.

Helpless and hopeless feelings are two of the most crippling aspects of the self-demeaning personality. Caring, insightful parental involvement is a powerful ally in your teenagers' battles against these personal-growth barriers.

6. Help your teenagers reduce their self-blame and direct their energies toward solving tasks. Though some self-demeaning teenagers blame others for their unhappiness, most hold themselves responsible. They internalize their anger. Even when they should be angry at someone else who's wronged them, they usually redirect that anger back to themselves. These adolescents routinely internalize their anger and blame, which leads to strong guilt. Each personal failure confirms their inadequacy, which reinforces their guilt and hopelessness.

You can be instrumental in helping your young people differentiate their mistakes, errors, sins and failings and the negative consequences they had little or no control over. They should feel responsible for failing an exam after they decided to attend a football game instead of studying. They should feel responsible for being late to work when they decided to go shopping with friends rather than take their own car. But there's no reason for them to blame themselves for their parents' divorce. With your help and support, your self-demeaning teenagers can release this huge burden of personal responsibility. Instead of feeling guilty for everything, they can learn to hold themselves accountable for only their own actions.

Encourage your young people to concentrate less on blame and fault and more on solving tasks. Even though it's important for adolescents to learn from their mistakes and correct their destructive behavior patterns, self-demeaning adolescents are too focused on their wrongdoings. Help them become more task-oriented. When something goes wrong, encourage them to think about how to correct the situation rather than who made the mistake.

"It doesn't matter who spilled the paint; we have a job to do. Let's work together to clean up this mess."

"Blaming yourself for the brakes failing isn't going to do any good now, Phil. Let's work out a transportation schedule for the time your car is in the repair shop."

Placing emphasis on the task that needs to be accomplished suggests you accept your teenagers and are willing to help them accomplish what needs to be done.

Self-blaming and repressed anger are destructive forces common to self-demeaning teenagers. You can help your adolescents turn these negative forces into positive task-directed energy.

7. Help these young people become less sensitive to criticism. Because self-demeaning teenagers already blame themselves and feel guilty, they have few defenses against others' criticism and judgment. They believe all criticisms or accusations aimed at them. They internalize all this negative input because it reinforces what they already believe about themselves. These young people don't possess the inner strengths necessary to evaluate, resist and reject untrue or unwarranted accusations. To evaluate and resist those kinds of accusations requires self-esteem, self-confidence and psychological energy. Self-demeaning adolescents don't possess these self-valuing characteristics.

You have a lot of control of and influence on your home's atmosphere. You can establish a positive, supportive environment or a negative, destructive atmosphere. Control your attitudes, words and actions. Give fewer criticisms and avoid making accusations. Try to actively support your family members. Though brothers and sisters are typically negative and critical toward one another, help your children lessen the frequency and intensity of their disparaging remarks.

When your self-demeaning son is criticized or faces a difficult accusation, encourage him to discuss his feelings with you. Let him talk while you listen. Try to respond to the pain you hear. Let him express his view of what happened. Support his efforts to explain his opinions and perspective. Help him accept his part of the responsibility without accepting any overwhelming guilt and self-condemnation.

As your self-demeaning teenagers become less sensitive to criticism, they gain the personal strengths that can help them mature. You can be a primary source of support for your young people's efforts to grow.

8. Encourage your teenagers to be more self-reliant. Independence is difficult for these adolescents to develop. Since they have no confidence in their abilities and strengths, they find no reason to rely on themselves. Self-demeaning teenagers believe they must trust someone stronger, wiser, older or better to direct them or take care of them. Sometimes they depend on fate or chance.

Christian self-demeaning adolescents often exhibit an unhealthy reliance on God. This dependency is unhealthy because they treat God like a magician who takes care of every need, even if the adolescent is capable of handling the situation. For example, they may ask God to help them pick the right color of hair ribbon or tell them which jacket to buy. This type of reliance on God doesn't stimulate personal growth and spiritual maturity. It assures self-demeaning teenagers they're inadequate and incompetent.

Help your teenagers grow in self-reliance. Work with them to identify their strengths and competencies. When they accomplish a task or overcome a difficult hurdle, reinforce their efforts. Tell them you're proud of them and help them congratulate themselves. When you see them work independently instead of asking for assistance, bring it to their attention. Help them recognize their growth toward increasing self-reliance so they can experience pride in their independence.

Self-demeaning adolescents are convinced they're personally inadequate. Helping them grow toward increasing self-reliance is a powerful gift you can offer your young people.

9. Help your teenagers feel they belong in your family. Belonging is one of the fundamental human psychological needs. The family is the first and most important group children sense they belong to. The way they seek to belong and the degree to which they secure their belonging has a great impact on their self-concept. Feeling insecure can devastate individuals' self-esteem and security.

Adolescents and children will do virtually anything to ensure that they belong. Their first attempts are positive efforts. They offer their positive, unique qualities, talents and skills in an attempt to be valued and included in the family unit. These positive attempts are largely unconscious but still purposeful.

If their positive efforts fail, adolescents turn to less positive or destructive efforts to get attention and a position in the family. For self-demeaning teenagers, negative attention is better than none at all. These young people may be disruptive, slow, negative and even destructive if that's the only way they can get recognition. These young people can find extremely negative ways to belong in their families.

Reinforce your self-demeaning teenagers' positive behavior. Ignore their negative behavior. When ignoring is impossible, strive to remove your negative reinforcement of their destructive and irritating actions. Remember, in these cases punishment actually increases the chances of their negative behavior continuing.

Find positive actions to reinforce.

"You sure had a good idea about how to prune the fruit tree."

"I really enjoyed your company on our shopping trip."

"Your sense of humor is delightful. You make our home so much more fun for all of us."

By encouraging their positive ways of belonging, you diminish the intensity and frequency of their negative behaviors.

You can help your teenagers find positive ways of establishing security in the family unit. By encouraging their positive approaches, you help your young people diminish their self-demeaning attitudes.

10. Support your children's friendships with teenagers who tend to build healthy relationships. Peer relationships are extremely important to an adolescent. Acceptance in specific peer groups and approval from selected friends are among a teenager's most highly prized experiences. The peer groups and teenagers selected by your young people powerfully impact how they develop through adolescence. You'll notice some friends have a positive effect on your children while others produce a negative effect. When you care about your children, you want to guide them into friendships that stimulate them positively. It's wise to realize you can't push certain relationships with much vigor or your teenagers will react in the opposite direction. Selection of friends is a common issue in parent-teenager conflicts. Your gentle encouragement of healthy friendships and cautious discouragement of less favorable relationships is difficult but important.

Aggressive, competitive and unhealthy power-oriented adolescents often intensify the negative tendencies of your self-demeaning young people. Close association with these personality types depreciates your teenagers' self-esteem and reinforces withdrawal and dependency. Self-demeaning young people form their healthiest relationships with responsible teenagers and power-oriented adolescents who are extremely caring. These young people are less likely to reinforce your self-demeaning teenagers' negative traits. These friendships actually stimulate your self-demeaning adolescent's growth and self-respect. Since people we relate to impact our attitudes, actions and feelings about ourselves, you need to guide your self-demeaning adolescents into healthy friendships and associations.

11. Seek to ensure an accurate, healthy theology of Jesus Christ for your teenagers. Idealism is an important characteristic of adolescence. Teenagers tend to make certain adults heroes and seek to emulate them. Young people believe they gain personal significance by acting like these special people.

Christian young people naturally idealize Jesus Christ (as they should) and seek to be like him. Jesus is an appropriate, positive identity to emulate. But many adolescents know Jesus only by what they read of him in the Bible and from what they hear ministers, teachers, other adults and peers say about him. Some young people form a partial, incomplete image of Jesus Christ. And sometimes this image contains significantly incorrect and unhealthy personality characteristics adolescents identify with. Self-demeaning teenagers are particularly vulnerable to incorporating these misunderstandings into their own personality because of their dependency on others and hesitancy to trust their own judgment and thinking.

These young people strongly defend their self-depreciating attitudes when they see Jesus as self-demeaning. Some misunderstand his meekness and love. They confuse Jesus' meekness with weakness. They mistakenly think Jesus is a "nice" person rather than a strong, assertive, loving individual.

You need to know what image your children have of Jesus Christ. During home Bible studies and spontaneous discussions, listen to what they say about who Jesus is. Then correct their misperceptions. Work with your teenagers to develop a positive, accurate image of Jesus Christ for them to emulate.

12. Help your self-demeaning young people accept God's love. With all our awareness of psychological principles and attendance to intellectual sophistication, it is vital we don't lose sight of our central healing source. There's absolutely nothing more healing or releasing than direct confrontation with God's love. Spiritual and psychological wholeness can't be attained without God's love.

Self-demeaning teenagers desperately need the freedom and energy resulting from opening themselves to receive God's care. Pray for your children and seek ways to expose them to God's love. Regularly attend church together as a family. Encourage your children's involvement in Sunday school, church youth groups and retreats. Help your children develop comfortable relationships with your minister, the youth director and other Christian adults by including these people in your family activities. Establish Bible study times and pray at home. One of your most vital tasks as a parent is to help your self-demeaning children experience and respond to God's love for them.

13. Patiently continue expressing love to your teenagers. Self-demeaning young people typically sabotage your efforts to love and encourage them. To accept love means risking rejection; to respond to encouragement means risking failure. These teenagers fear rejection and failure and may go to extremes to avoid both.

These teenagers usually try to get you to give up on them. They initiate behavior intended to frustrate your efforts. When you give up and withdraw your love and support, these teenagers have no one to help them.

Self-demeaning adolescents need you to be stronger and more tenacious than they are. They need your love to be stronger than their self-directed anger. Be patient when you seek to help. Allow God the time he needs to use your and others' efforts to help your teenagers.

CHAPTER SIX

The Dependent Personality

Dependent teenagers model behavior typical of the old dictum, "Children should be seen and not heard." Some adults still think all children should follow this rule. They believe the pre-adult years are for silence, staying out of the way and not causing any problems. These adults think children should receive attention at their parents' and other adults' convenience since their needs remain secondary to adults' needs.

All adolescents experience the dependence-independence conflict as they move through adolescence. When young people encounter excessive problems or fail this developmental task, they become increasingly dependent. Dependent teenagers have particular difficulty gaining personal strength and independence. Through their behavior these young people say: "I'm a weak person with little personal worth. But I admire others and need their support to feel secure in this world."

Dependent teenagers primarily fear they'll be inadequate or fail if placed in positions of power, responsibility or leadership. Therefore, they prefer to rely on someone else who'll assume responsibility or adopt the leadership role. They avoid personal accountability by depending on others. They truly believe in their helplessness and reinforce this belief each time they avoid leadership or responsibility.

► *Development of the Dependent Personality*

Gaining a strong sense of independence is one of adolescents' essential developmental tasks as they grow successfully toward adulthood. Young people must begin to believe in themselves as individuals who need less and less advice or guidance. Because dependent personality types tend to develop more slowly, they don't grow toward this independence. They're overly agreeable, easily influenced and more than willing to follow another's lead. Usually they're easy children to parent, but some may experience difficulty with their social and personal adjustments. And if these needy teenagers don't receive help, they're destined to have serious future problems. Understanding their problems' source is often the first step toward knowing how we can help. Here are some experiences that most commonly contribute to adolescents developing a dependent personality type:

1. Lack of nurture and support. Failure to nurture and support children early in their life stifles their ability to develop strength and independence later. Many tragic case histories of dependent personalities reveal insecure teenagers and adults who never received adequate love, affection, touch, conversation or other forms of caring during their childhood. Instead of strengthening or toughening these children, this lack of human warmth weakens development of their self-esteem and confidence and destroys their trust in themselves and the external world. Lack of adequate care and attention during early months and years deprives people of the internal building blocks necessary to establish enduring personality strengths. This failure to nurture also fosters dependency as children grow older.

2. Discouragement. Adults sometimes discourage adolescents' attempts to develop and express their personality strengths. Parents may react negatively to their children's early assertive expressions of their opinions, ideas and feelings. Some parents may misperceive these early expressions of personal strength as sinful pride, while others may feel personally threatened or uneasy when confronted with their children's self-assertions.

Many parents require their children's behavior to be excessively well-ordered and structured. Intense emphasis on rules, routine, a controlled noise level and how things should be done properly can stifle ingenuity, creativity and spontaneity. Rigid behavioral controls can thwart children's willingness to risk, accept responsibility and take initiative. These problems may intensify if these children experience the same rigid structure in their classrooms, Sunday school classes, child-care facilities or other supervised settings.

3. Dependency mistaken for spiritual meekness. Sometimes young people's timidity, insecurity and excessive modesty are mistakenly reinforced as positive examples of spiritual meekness. Remember, spiritual meekness never implies weakness. Unfortunately, some testimonies of God's faithfulness falsely glorify human passivity—which is quite different from an energized, faithful patience while trusting in God's leading.

Patiently waiting on God isn't passive. It's not motionless. Neither is it without action and direction. Read what James writes about patience: "Be patient, then, brothers, until the Lord's coming. See how the farmer waits for the land to yield its valuable crop and how patient he is for the autumn and spring rains. You too, be patient and stand firm, because the Lord's coming is near . . . Brothers, as an example of patience in the face of suffering, take the prophets who spoke in the name of the Lord. As you know, we consider blessed those who have persevered. You have heard of Job's perseverance and have seen what the Lord finally brought about. The Lord is full of compassion and mercy" (James 5:7-8, 10-11).

Certainly, farmers aren't passive while waiting for their fields to yield crops. They work busily at many tasks while "patiently" waiting for their harvest. The prophets surely weren't idle as they delivered their messages of what was to come. They persisted despite continual suffering and persecution.

We dare not squelch our children's spirits. We mustn't sabotage their drive toward individuality. If we discourage assertive individuality as an unhealthy spiritual value, we may encourage our children's development of dependent personalities.

4. Comparisons. Some adolescents have been negatively impacted by their own misperceptions of themselves or others' reactions to them. Psychologists have studied the intricate relationships between brothers and sisters as one of the most powerful sources of influence upon children's developing personalities. Children naturally compare themselves with their siblings. They learn to value or devalue themselves largely according to how they think they compare with the other children in their family.

"I don't think I'm as smart as my older brother."

"I don't understand it. I'm nowhere near as popular as my younger sister."

"I'm a lot stronger and faster than my brother."

Comparisons young people make with friends and other peers also have a strong impact. A major danger is that many children make grievous mistakes in their personal perceptions. For example, many teenage beauty-contest winners honestly evaluate their physical appearance as average or below average. One junior high boy told his teacher he thought of himself as a dumb student. Compared with his older brother who had a straight-"A" average, he incorrectly thought his "B+" average was worthless. Many second-string quarterbacks struggle with self-depreciating attitudes because of their inaccurately low perceptions of their athletic prowess. They feel worthless because they're not "the best" in their schools.

As you listen to teenagers talk about their childhoods, families and early-life experiences, listen carefully for indicators of their reality perception. Does what they say fit with your knowledge about them and your family? Are there inconsistencies between their self-evaluations and what they've actually accomplished? Significant misperceptions and erroneous self-evaluations during childhood can have dramatic, far-reaching effects on personality formation during adolescence and into adulthood.

5. Self-reinforcement. Dependency can become self-reinforcing behavior. Remember, since using dependency as a defense mechanism reduces young people's anxiety, there is an increased chance that their dependent behavior will repeat itself. Defense mechanisms are used because they work well. Forming dependent relationships with individuals perceived as strong and responsible creates a sense of security for some young people. During adolescence when there is so much personal trauma and anxiety related to social situations, dependency may become an effective maneuver to reduce anxiety and feel safe.

6. Good experiences. Dependent people can successfully fulfill several different interpersonal functions. Many of these teenagers have had good experiences with being dependent throughout their childhood. They'd argue that the world needs followers as well as leaders, and there can't be leaders without a plentiful supply of followers. These young people have found value through following and attaching their loyalty to others. They feel most comfortable when they support others' efforts rather than promote their own cause.

Energetic followers and supporters gain much reinforcement from following others. Appreciated and reinforced for the support and help given their leader, these adolescents experience external praise and internal good feelings that promote their dependent behavior. Evidence of these social patterns suggests early development of dependent personalities.

► Healthy Forms of the Dependent Personality

A central issue for all adolescents' development is the movement from being dependent on others toward greater equality in their relationships. When this movement stalls, slows or is non-existent, a dependent personality probably exists. There are several healthy, positive expressions of this personality orientation (as long as individuals don't become excessive or overly rigid in their dependency).

Each of the following examples exemplifies primarily healthy, adaptive forms of the dependent personality type. All three relate well to others, aren't destructive in their relationships and are pleasant and enjoyable to be around. The "follower," "admirer" and "imitator" are often productive, healthy expressions of the dependent social orientation.

The Follower. Fifteen-year-old Ed appears to be a typically involved sophomore in high school. When he and his church youth group recently attended their denomination's large regional youth conference, Ed participated in as many activities and meetings as he possibly could. He was pleasant, his attitude was cheerful and the kids who met him at the conference seemed to like him. Outwardly, Ed related quite well in the large group. He also supported others in the small groups. During one of the small group sessions, several of his new acquaintances used words such as "happy," "encouraging," "good-natured" and "helpful" to describe him. But his youth leader noticed that Ed revealed little about himself or his ideas when any personal talk occurred.

Ed grew up in a strict family environment. His parents administered fair discipline and taught him traditional values. As the sixth of eight children, Ed had little opportunity to exercise his leadership muscles. Instead he learned to depend on others who were older and stronger. Relying on others and following their lead resulted in good experiences, positive relationships and pleasurable feelings of belonging and acceptance. His mother and all the children attended church regularly, and his dad joined them occasionally.

Since both parents had to work, everyone shared household responsibilities. The children were raised to cooperate and help one another. If anyone shirked his or her duties, group pressure became intense. However, the family atmosphere was usually pleasant and happy. There was ample love and commitment from each parent and mutual caring among the children. Aside from the typical sibling rivalry, brothers and sisters usually supported one another, and they became good friends as they grew into adolescence.

Ed learned how to adapt to others from his childhood and early adolescence in his family. As he advanced in school, he continued relating to others in much the same way he learned at home. He was socially successful at school and in his neighborhood, and he was also popular in his church youth group. Ed was known for his encouragement, support and loyalty. Though he hesitated to offer his own opinions, he eagerly affirmed someone else's.

Ed had found dependence a comfortable, successful way to interact with others. He gained his acceptance and belonging through following the lead of those around him. He also learned to believe in others' strengths more than his own. He found meaning in being a supportive, loyal follower.

The Admirer. Esther entered counseling at age 15, when she was a sophomore. Although she wasn't in a crisis or severe trouble, she gained from the experience as her counselor helped her search for ways to prevent more serious future problems. Although many of her friends described her as easy to get along with, Esther's counselor saw her as passive and dependent.

The youngest of two daughters, Esther was only 3 years old when her parents divorced. Both girls lived with their mother, but their father visited them regularly once or twice a month. As a single parent, Esther's mother was determined her daughters would grow up highly valuing responsibility. She firmly enforced all rules and required prompt completion of routine chores. Strict and demanding, she succeeded in teaching her children the importance of responsible behavior, but her approach partially sabotaged her purpose. Her strength and intensity overpowered Esther and her sister. Thus, Esther learned to take responsibility for her behavior, but her personal strength was crushed. Unable to produce the inner strength necessary for initiating her own actions and desires, she learned to identify with and depend on someone else she perceived as powerful.

Esther's stepfather, who entered her life when she was 7 years old, unwittingly intensified her dependency with his role modeling. A kind, generous man, he passively accepted Esther's mother's decisions about family finances, social life and vacations. He happily allowed her to manage his wages, and each weekend he responded readily to her "Honey-do" list. Unconsciously, Esther's stepfather proved to her that life is best when you can depend on someone who's strong, capable and trustworthy.

Since she was 11 or 12 years old, Esther has periodically attached herself to one or two special people she deeply respects and admires. Even though she doesn't understand why she's attracted to certain people, she's selected several teachers, church youth leaders, Sunday school teachers and some of her mother's adult friends as special. She's also elevated several of her peers to this exalted position. Boys who show a lot of masculine bravado particularly catch Esther's attention. She's attracted four older boyfriends, each physically, athletically or socially more capable than her. She's especially drawn to responsible, power-oriented and competitive individuals because of their strength and self-confidence.

When Esther admires someone, she's a "one-girl fan club." She tells everyone how great her hero is. Through her identification with the other person's power and influence, she also feels powerful and influential. By sharing her admiration for another, she elicits enthusiasm and exuberance from others. She then identifies with the admiration they experience and accepts it for herself. Esther handles these complex personal dynamics so successfully that everyone feels better. She feels stronger by caboosing on another's glory. Her admired one feels better because of the increased notoriety and respect her relationship brings. And others feel better because they've affirmed another person.

Esther is generally liked and accepted by other teenagers. They enjoy having her around, but her peers usually don't have strong feelings about her. She's described as "sweet," "kind," "nice" and "a good person." She's easy to have around, fits in well with most groups and adapts readily to different types of people. Unfortunately, these same positive qualities create some of her potential problems.

Even though Esther is passive and dependent, she's successful because she isn't extreme enough to be self-destructive. The goal of her counseling is to help her find, develop and rely on her own inner strengths.

The Imitator. At age 19, Sean started seeing a professional counselor. Upon graduating high school, he'd taken a full-time job as a plumber's helper, which he held for a year. Then he entered the local community college. Halfway through the first semester, he encountered an impasse. Unable. to concentrate, he dropped two of his courses, thinking this would relieve some of the tension. A few weeks later he could no longer force himself to even attend his remaining classes. He was depressed, anxious and temporarily incapable of coping with even the slightest stress. He felt this way for almost two weeks before his first counseling session. But in six weeks of twice-weekly sessions, Sean felt much stronger. With his newly acquired self-confidence, he enrolled in and successfully completed his classes during the next semester.

What caused this temporary break in Sean's effective functioning during his late adolescence? With no indication that he was headed for trouble, why did this happen to him? After a few counseling sessions with Sean, his therapist could answer these questions for him and his parents and help them understand the effect of his personality development.

Sean was the second of three boys in his stable, middle-class family. His older brother had always been an excellent student, and his younger brother was an outstanding athlete. From elementary school, Sean couldn't claim to be "best" in any activities that typically affirm teenagers' self-esteem. He felt outclassed by both his brothers. It was bad enough that he couldn't match his older brother's straight-"A" average, but he felt totally humiliated when his younger brother surpassed him in athletic accomplishments. By the middle of eighth grade, Sean realized he couldn't compete with either brother and win.

Another major factor influenced Sean's personality development. When he was 8 years old, his mother experienced a deep depression. Because she was suicidal, her doctors hospitalized her for six weeks. Her outpatient psychotherapy continued another two years until she'd overcome her serious depression. During her illness Sean worried about her excessively. When she refused to get out of bed, when she was angry and complaining and when she didn't have enough energy to complete her household tasks, Sean blamed himself. He felt guilty, thinking he ought to be able to do something about her situation. These thoughts and feelings led him to even deeper self-doubts.

Sean handled his discouragement and guilt by forming a

dependent personality. However, his personality orientation was somewhat different from the teenagers' earlier in this section. Instead of becoming a follower or an admirer of others, Sean began imitating people he respected and valued. Like Ed's and Esther's social orientations, his adaptation was healthy because it wasn't sufficiently extreme to destroy his social relationships. However, his own acute depression was a spinoff, resulting from his imitation. As he gained feelings of significance by imitating others' gestures, verbal characteristics and behaviors, he hindered his own identity's development. The natural pressures of moving from late adolescence to early adulthood created more stress than his limited identity could handle. His adaptive functioning broke down, and he regressed in an attempt to regain his psychological balance.

In junior high and early high school, Sean tried to imitate outstanding athletes and some other class leaders. He wore the same clothes, used the same language and participated in the same activities as they did, as much as possible. He became a keen observer and sometimes unconsciously replicated their actions, attitudes and interests. Even though this adaptation brought him some success and others' acceptance, he still felt empty and unfulfilled. At some level of consciousness, he realized he wasn't developing an identity uniquely his own.

During his high school junior and senior years, he identified with a group of heavy drug users. He dressed like they did, picked up their speech style, changed his personal habits to mirror theirs and then began using their drugs. Although at first he felt good about his acceptance in a new group of friends, he felt uneasy about giving up his loftier ambitions and ideals.

Late in his senior year Sean became involved in church and the youth group. He made a strong commitment to Christ. Sean's youth minister took special interest in him, spending much time counseling and discipling him. Sean developed great respect for this young adult. Because he meant so much to him, Sean naturally began imitating his youth minister, expressing his desire to be the person God wanted him to be. Though certainly a more positive role model than his drug-using buddies, his youth minister still wasn't the person God created Sean to be. Sean needed to seek his own identity. Instead of imitating those around him, Sean needed to discover his own way of uniquely reflecting God, in whose image he was created.

► Unhealthy Forms of the Dependent Personality

When dependency becomes excessive, teenagers' social adaptations cease to work well for them. Their perceptions of their inner weaknesses prevent them from establishing relationships based on their own strengths. Social contacts are characterized by adolescents' dependencies and thereby lose their ability to be healthy, well-balanced and nourishing. The following three case studies depict unhealthy, maladaptive forms of the dependent adolescent personality type.

The Helpless. For most of her life Rhonda has been the epitome of helplessness. Her social behavior expresses one overwhelming message, "I must have your advice, direction and strength, or I absolutely can't survive." Rhonda was a 17-year-old senior when she initiated therapy. She suffered severe anxiety attacks and had pervasive fears of being around people. She felt terribly alone and saw herself as isolated in an uncaring, dangerous world.

The immediate cause of her symptoms was readily evident. Her anxiety attacks began a few days after her boyfriend broke up with her. They'd been close, and she was extremely dependent on him. For the past two years she'd relied on him for almost everything she did. She used him to provide all her social needs, going out only when she could be with him. She could get passing grades only when she studied with him. She finally learned to drive only when he took time to teach her. Evenings and weekends when he couldn't be with her, she stayed home, bored, listless and unproductive.

When Rhonda started dating this young man, she slowly let go of her relationships with girlfriends. She stopped going out with them, didn't return their phone calls and avoided them at school and church in an attempt to spend more time with her boyfriend. Therefore, when she lost him, she no longer had others she could immediately turn to for support.

We can understand how Rhonda developed her helpless dependency if we look into her family dynamics and the childhood social experiences that affected her early life. Her father styled himself after the classic benevolent dictator. He found his pride in providing financially for his family and protecting them from harm. In return for these services, he required his family's trust, loyalty, obedience and dependency. Since their church heavily emphasized the husband's authority and wife's submission, Rhonda's mother gladly fulfilled the requirements. She vividly role modeled helpless dependency for her three daughters. Thus, Rhonda learned to associate helplessness with desirable femininity and appropriate Christian behavior.

Rhonda developed great skill at positioning herself in a helpless role with others. The youngest of three girls, she made good use of her older sisters' abilities and willingness to do things for her, many of which she could have done herself. As a result she began falsely believing in her helplessness. When she started school, she transferred her needy social behavior to this environment as well. Her teachers described her as "charming but passive." She'd successfully learned how to ask favors from others without making them resent her. And when her friends tired of her helpless demands, she'd find others happy to feel needed.

By the time she reached adolescence, Rhonda was especially adept at attracting power-oriented and responsible young people. The central basis for all her social relationships continued to be her helpless dependency. She felt included and accepted only when someone helped her. She experienced her own strengths only when she could pull helping responses from others through her display of weakness and helplessness.

The Gullible. From all appearances, 18-year-old Salvadore was making a positive adjustment to life throughout his mid-adolescence. Popular among his peers, he was also well-liked by his teachers and other adults. He'd always been friendly, warm and easy to get along with. But during his senior year, he began struggling with his inability to determine what was real. And his gullibility began interfering with his interactions with others.

In a family of seven children, Salvadore was the second-youngest. He was the younger of only two boys and received much love and attention from his mother and four older sisters. Because he was a cute, charming small child, Salvadore learned early to entice older children and adults to respond to him. He learned to get attention without doing anything constructive or helpful for either himself or others. He remained passive in his social relationships because everyone else was so willing to do all his work and carry responsibility for their relationship with him. Playing the role of the adorable child was all Salvadore had to do. He performed so well others were delighted to have him around.

Like most gullible people, Salvadore learned to work the system too well. He used his dependent relating style so often that he increasingly narrowed his range of possibilities for social responses. He slowly became utterly dependent on others to lead any of his interpersonal interactions. Encouraged by his protective home environment, he became overly trusting. No matter what others said, he believed them. And he would, without question, do almost anything anyone said he should.

Since others took care of most of his needs and wants, Salvadore developed few skills and no special abilities. There was virtually nothing he could do well or significantly better than others. He had no hobbies and his few efforts to do something constructive during his childhood were largely unsuccessful. This lack of success resulted in his discouragement and giving up. He learned not to trust himself. He discovered others were more skilled, interesting and often more correct than he was. This dependence on others and their abilities began early in his life.

Salvadore's adorable nature allowed him to progress through elementary school without any personal pain or interpersonal problems. As he moved through junior high, however, he began feeling empty and insecure. Still active and popular in his relationships with both his peers and adults, he internalized his pain and hid it beneath his charming exterior. Finally, during his senior year his internal void collapsed, and his growing expectations and needs for independent functioning in relationships broke through his thin defenses. His lack of confidence and minimal abilities and talents were inadequate to sustain him through late adolescence. Salvadore's personality development had stalled psychologically and socially at the pre-adolescent stage.

The most visible symptom of Salvadore's unhealthy personality development was his extremely gullible reaction to what others said or did. His friends had a great time when they wanted to get a reaction from him.

"Hey, Sal, are you ready for the English midterm today? You didn't know about it? Boy, are you in for it now!"

"Sal, you know that awesome cheerleader, Brenda? Well, she thinks you're something else. She really likes you. She wants you to ask her to homecoming next week."

"Gee, Sal, we better get home. I heard on the radio a big tornado is expected to strike any minute. We better leave and warn our families even if the principal won't let us out of school."

With no inner strength or confidence in his own thinking, Salvadore merely accepted being set up by his friends. Instead of evaluating the situation, Sal simply believed whatever anyone told him. Rather than think for himself about what was or wasn't real, he relied on what others said. Lacking the inner strength to disagree or question, he passively accepted what he was told. Even though these incidents were innocent and meant for fun, they intensified Salvadore's conviction that he was inferior and inadequate.

As each year passes, Salvadore's dependency becomes more inappropriate and increasingly maladaptive. His gullible style of social interaction increasingly evidences his inner weaknesses and personal ineptitude.

The Clinging Vine. Carmen was born to an unmarried teenage mother who elected to keep her child. The young mother lived with her own mother who'd divorced several years earlier. When Carmen was 2 years old, her grandmother developed breast cancer, underwent extensive surgery followed by eight months of chemotherapy and couldn't return to work. This unexpected illness and lack of

any extended family support forced Carmen's mother to work to support her small family. When the young mother finally recognized her inability to handle the combination of working, caring for her ill mother and mothering her toddler daughter, she placed Carmen in a receiving home, hoping to find acceptable adoptive parents for her.

Reacting to the instability and trauma surrounding her life, Carmen developed severe temper tantrums. Her behavior repelled potential adoptive parents, so she spent the next seven years living in a series of foster homes. Several of these homes offered her love and structure, and none of her foster parents was abusive. But most families provided little more than food, clothing and shelter.

Shortly after her ninth birthday, Carmen was placed with an unusually loving, nurturing couple that also had a 13-year-old natural daughter. Almost immediately, Carmen felt she'd "come home." Her temper tantrums subsided, and she began feeling more and more secure with this new family. After 10 months her foster parents applied to adopt Carmen. And by the time she was 11 years old, she had a new mother, father and sister who were legally hers.

As Carmen's temper tantrums disappeared, a new behavior characterized her social interactions. She began attaching herself to one friend at a time. While dependent on that one person, Carmen cared nothing about anyone else. She wanted to do everything with that one individual, and became depressed and obviously upset when that person did things with others. Her continual need for contact and attention strained her social relationships. Most of her friends couldn't tolerate this much intensity for more than a few months, so they withdrew, usually with some form of meanness to discourage Carmen's clinging. But without fail, she'd enter another mutual pact of loyalty and friendship with someone else a few days after one of these traumatic episodes ended.

Besides clinging to her peers, Carmen developed a similar pattern of clinging to adults. For two years following her adoption Carmen clung tightly to her new foster parents. When she finally felt secure in that relationship, she began parceling out her loyalty among her parents' adult friends, her teachers, Sunday school teachers and neighbors. These hand-picked adults temporarily provided her with further security and stability until they, too, disappointed her with their imperfection in meeting all her needs.

When she was 15 years old, Carmen's parents took her to a professional therapist who specialized in treating adolescents. During the first few sessions the therapist discovered that her clinging-vine pattern of social interaction began in her extremely insecure early childhood. Her repeated loss of loved ones during her early years reinforced her belief that there are no stable relationships she can depend on. As most children do, Carmen internalized the problem—she blamed herself. She thought there must be something terribly wrong with her that made her unlovable and made others leave her.

Carmen's response to this feeling of inadequacy was to tighten her grip on anyone who befriended or showed interest in her. She exaggerated small signals of liking into commitments of loyalty and exclusiveness. Her clinging was an attempt to control and possess all the other person's time and resources for the purpose of befriending him or her.

► *Effects of Dependent Behavior on Others*

Each of the eight personality types in this book elicits both positive and negative reactions from others. Usually, behavior intensity determines whether these reactions are favorable or unhappy. Others' reactions to the intensity of a dependent teenager's behavior are usually quite clear and logically fit the needs the dependent behavior expresses.

A "follower" such as Ed often elicits strength and leadership from others. This dependency maneuver especially affects power-oriented and responsible people. An "admirer" such as Esther often stimulates self-respect and self-affirmation in the individuals he or she respects. And in return, these people enjoy being around an individual who admires and "looks up" to them. An "imitator" can have the same impact on others that an admirer does since imitation is one of the finest forms of a compliment. If taken to an extreme, however, an imitating teenager may draw irritation and rejection from others.

Even an unhealthy form of dependency draws positive responses, especially from responsible and power-oriented individuals. Many people want to provide some form of help, a friendly response or nurturing support to an individual who is dependent in the relationship. Some need to offer direction or advice to an adolescent who appears helpless. Others may extend sympathetic understanding plus offer support or reassurance to a young person who behaves dependently. These positive responses usually turn negative, however, when the dependent behavior takes an unhealthy form or becomes maladaptive in its intensity.

Like the unhealthy self-demeaning teenager, a dependent adolescent sometimes refuses others' help. When offers of assistance repeatedly fail to bring a positive response or change, the helping individuals often react with frustration, anger and withdrawal. In Salvadore's example, we saw how a gullible individual can bring a derisive, "making fun of" reaction from friends. In this way "gullible" Salvadore is similar to the clown type of masochist in the self-destructive personality type in Chapter 5. Rather than confront or question the social relationships offered by others, Sal merely accepts the dependent role his friends have chosen for him.

As a teenager's dependent behavior becomes more extreme, others usually choose one of two responses. Most finally push the dependent teenager away or withdraw to regain their personal freedom. Others, especially those who are less competitive, power-oriented or responsible, may initially try to foster even more dependency. When this happens, an unhealthy symbiotic relationship develops that's destructive to both people. Each individual reinforces the other's unhealthiness. Usually in these cases, the healthier of the two individuals finally rebels against the other's controls and pulls away from the relationship.

One clue to identifying a particular personality orientation is the most common reaction from others. When the primary responses outlined in this section characteristize reactions given to your adolescent, he or she may be a dependent teenager.

► *Guidelines for Parenting Dependent Adolescents*

As a parent of dependent teenagers, you're in a delicate position. Your children are struggling to gain independence from you, and you want to help them with this developmental task. But your assistance seems to enmesh them in further dependency. You may feel frustrated, but you can help your dependent adolescents many ways.

1. Carefully observe what your teenagers say through their actions. Teenagers function developmentally between children and adults. Even though they can discuss their inner experiences, they're more likely to act out their feelings, attitudes and opinions. You can usually discover more about your teenagers by observing their behavior than by listening to their words. As you watch what they do and how they do it, recall past experiences that could have contributed to your children's dependent personality development. Your awareness of their past helps you understand what you observe now.

Your careful observation of your teenagers' behaviors can provide deeper understanding of their feelings and thoughts. Donny's lack of interest in school and his sudden drop in grades might say: "I've missed Dad so much since the divorce. I don't want to try anymore." Marcia's exuberance and eagerness to help in the kitchen might say: "I'm so happy Bill asked me out for Friday night. I want everyone to be as happy as I am."

Behavior motivated by dependency needs is often exhibited in young people's desires for approval, imitation of others' actions or reliance on another's directions. By carefully observing your teenagers' behaviors and relating them to their pasts, you gain your best understanding of why your teenagers act the way they do.

2. Treat your teenagers with respect. Your teenagers learn how to see themselves largely from the way the family treats them. Dependent young people usually don't highly regard themselves. Nor do they typically recognize their personal strengths. These adolescents believe they're weak and incompetent. They choose to depend on someone else rather than rely on their abilities. Often they idealize one or two people and constantly seek their company. Dependent teenagers experience success and adequacy by associating and identifying with others who are ambitious, popular or successful.

An effective way to help your dependent young people is to consistently treat them with respect. Tell them you think they're valuable. Help them realize that what they do or how well they perform isn't nearly as important to you as who they are. Spontaneously express your love and high regard when they've done nothing to earn it. "Felippe, I want you to know how proud I am to be your dad."

Show your teenagers respect by recognizing and considering their needs. Think of the various needs common to adolescents and respond appropriately. A closed bedroom door may reflect your teenager's need for privacy. It may say, "I need to be alone right now." Respect your own courtesy rule and knock before entering another's space.

Remember, the way people feel about themselves usually reflects the way others treat them. Dependent adolescents need to increase their self-respect. You can help them accomplish this goal by offering them the same respect you expect from them.

3. Encourage your teenagers to develop inner strengths and self-reliance. The central issue with dependent adolescents is their lack of confidence in their strengths and skills. They don't believe they can function adequately in life. Challenges and opportunities normal for most teenagers seemingly overwhelm these young people. Fear, shame, guilt, panic and feelings of inadequacy often cripple these adolescents while their peers operate comfortably in similar situations.

To protect themselves from the weight of life's demands, these young people depend on others' strengths. They maneuver themselves into positions in which others feel they must watch over them. This positioning reinforces both their own and others' images of them as inadequate and protects them from further stress. Dependent teenagers strive to convince others they can't handle life without excessive help, support and protection. As a parent, you may be a primary target for this display of dependency.

Refuse to accept your dependent teenagers' perceived inadequacies. Without arguing, support the development of your teenagers' inner strengths. Give your young people responsibilities that stretch their concepts of what they can accomplish. Don't move too quickly. Enhance their chances of success by enlisting their help with things you know they can accomplish. Planning an evening meal, reorganizing the garage, taking care of errands, helping younger siblings find lost items and scheduling a family outing are tasks that exercise these young people's self-reliance.

Dependent adolescents want their parents to rescue them when things become frightening or difficult. Unless the situation is extreme, refuse to save them. Don't reinforce their belief in their helplessness.

Fifteen-year-old Marty was house-sitting for some vacationing neighbors. Since he was afraid he hadn't done things correctly, he wanted his parents to do a final check to make sure everything was okay before the neighbors returned. His parents gently refused, telling him they were confident he'd managed things well.

Dependent young people such as Marty need your support and assistance to build their confidence in their personal strengths. Your trust and confidence in their abilities can have a powerful, positive impact on their self-confidence.

4. Allow your young people to make mistakes while they're still in the supportive home environment. When you see people you love experience failure and negative consequences for their mistakes and poor choices, you hurt too. You feel especially bad when your dependent teenagers, who already struggle with self-doubts and low self-esteem, fail. But do you help them by unnecessarily protecting them from reality? By shielding them, you essentially give them a false impression of the world we live in. They mistakenly learn they can make unwise decisions and proceed carelessly without negative consequences. That type of unrealistic concept can seriously thwart them for the rest of their lives. Part of your task as a parent is to equip your children to live effective lives in the real world. Just as your relationship with God equips you to live effectively for him, God expects you to help your children do the same.

Overprotection teaches dependent adolescents they're inadequate. When you reinforce your teenagers' false perceptions of their abilities to learn and grow, you breed more dependency in personality structures that are already overly dependent. Remember Marty, the young man in the previous guideline? While Marty was house-sitting, he forgot to water several plants, and they died. He also neglected the goldfish, and they became ill. Since his parents didn't cover for him, he had to face his employers and his own irresponsibility. Even though his experience was extremely painful, it was better for him to learn the importance of carefully following directions now, rather than later when his failure might affect a career.

Florence's parents encouraged her to organize the family's Sunday picnic. She did an admirable job; she remembered everything—except something to drink. When Florence's parents gave her responsibility for the picnic, they didn't remind her of the details. The family went on the picnic and had a great time, even though everyone was thirsty. With her family's support, Florence learned she could handle a large responsibility by making a list and checking it carefully to be sure she collected all the necessary items.

You don't want your children to experience pain. But a little pain now may prevent more serious consequences later when the security of parents and home isn't available.

5. Discipline in ways that enhance personal accountability and self-respect. Think of your discipline as more than behavior control. The way you discipline your children impacts their self-concepts; it affects how they see the world and reinforces or alters their attitudes toward authority figures and others. The Bible clearly supports parental authority, but you need to vary your methods of God-given authority to meet each of your children's personality needs. Since dependent teenagers already believe they're inadequate and possess little self-worth, be extremely careful that your discipline method doesn't reinforce these negative attitudes. Don't demean or belittle them. These adolescents experience harsh, authoritarian discipline methods as further proof that they're hopelessly inadequate. This severe discipline makes these young people feel even more helpless. They fear they can never become worthwhile or valuable.

Discipline your dependent teenagers with logical, natural consequences that help these young people feel more responsible for their actions. When you discipline with consequences, you effectively gain control of behavior without destroying fragile self-concepts. While punishment places responsibility on the adults, logical, natural consequences place responsibility directly on the adolescents.

"Tony, you got home an hour after your curfew last night. Your actions tell me you're having trouble handling your freedom responsibly. You won't go out next weekend, so you'll have time to think about your situation. We'll talk Monday evening, and you can tell me what you think you can handle. Then we'll decide what to do."

"Sandy, your grades took an obvious nose dive this quarter. The teachers' comments indicate that your main problem is incomplete homework assignments. We'll reserve the hour between 7 and 8 p.m. each school night for your homework and studies, and we'll see how that system works. At the end of next quarter we'll evaluate this study program."

Each of these approaches uses logical consequences that make sense in relation to the teenager's behavior. The changes instituted by the parent resulted from hearing what his or her young person's behavior said and then responding directly to that message.

Remember to discipline with concern rather than anger. Use your discipline to teach and train as well as control. Dependent teenagers need your assistance. One way you can help your young people develop confidence is by disciplining with care and instruction on how to improve. This way your teenagers can learn valuable lessons about personal responsibility.

6. Communicate acceptance to your teenagers and let them know you love them just the way they are. Young people who continually underrate themselves benefit greatly from consistent

messages that others value them. They need continual assurance that you're delighted to have them in your family. Belonging is a central human need, and these teenagers find
little in themselves to assure them that they belong. They
passively involve themselves in family activities and pleasantly go along with what others want or suggest. But they
never initiate anything on their own nor do they invest
much of themselves in what's happening. Therefore, they
gain little in return. With so little involvement or investment
of their time or feelings, they receive little assurance that
their family members appreciate their value.

Take the initiative to involve your dependent young people in your family's interactions. Invite them to help you
with your projects and chores. Suggest doing something
together just to have fun. Ask to join them in their room,
and chat about the day you both had. Your willingness to
initiate activities and your consistent approaches for contact
help your young people believe they're important to you.

You can also help your dependent teenagers by pointing
out any of their personal characteristics you especially enjoy.
These young people need to know that you appreciate them,
and they benefit even more from knowing what you specifically like about them.

"Lamont, your neat sense of humor and quick wit keep
our home an interesting and fun place to be. We sure enjoy
having you around."

"This place wouldn't be the same without your quiet way
of helping and loving. I think you bring out the best in all
of us, Paula."

Make sure you specify real characteristics. Don't be phony.
Help them identify their best personal traits, then encourage
them to develop them further.

Dependent teenagers need to know that you enjoy and value them for who they are. Your actions and words can reassure these young people of their valued place in the family.

7. Help your young people develop their individual differences.
Dependent teenagers don't value their individuality. They
devalue themselves to the point they must rely on another's
strength for their personal significance. They see their individuality more as a threat to their okayness than an asset

they can nurture and develop. Often these adolescents are unaware of their unique qualities. When you comment on specific personal characteristics you admire, they may be surprised. They honestly believe there's nothing intrinsically worthwhile or noteworthy about them.

After helping them identify what differentiates them from others, encourage them to feel positive about those differences. Your consistent expressions of appreciation and enjoyment help them begin valuing their individuality.

Support your dependent teenagers' attempts to express their unique qualities. Reinforce their forms of self-expression and inventiveness, especially in less important areas such as dress, hair styles and music. Tolerate your teenagers' less offensive forms of self-expression as part of developing a healthy adolescent identity. As teenagers grow into mid- and late adolescence, the more extreme expressions of their individuality begin subsiding. Console yourself that most young people gradually return to values, interests, beliefs and activities closely related to their parents'.

Encourage your dependent teenagers to identify and develop their special interests and talents. Help them experiment. Let them try several musical instruments. Suggest they take photography, mechanics, graphic-arts or performing-arts classes. Encourage their involvement in student government, science projects and sports. Focus on their enjoyment rather than their expertise. Ask them what they like, and let them choose things that stimulate their interests.

Dependent teenagers need to discover what makes them different from others. They need to realize that their unique qualities help make them special to you. Show them how their individuality adds to the family unit. Help them see how their good characteristics contribute value to the family.

8. Refuse to believe your teenagers are helpless. Many dependent young people have convinced themselves they're helpless. They honestly believe they don't possess the inner strengths necessary to be significant people. They recognize personal strength only through their identification with and dependence on others.

Dependent teenagers desperately need your refusal to accept their helplessness. They need you to believe in their inner strengths; and that is hard work. Each time you push and prod your dependent teenagers to take risks, you have to overcome their resistance. These adolescents try to convince you to give up on them by failing. Be sensitive to your children's real limits, but patiently encourage them to try new tasks.

You can help your teenagers find and develop their inner strengths.

• Refuse to believe them when they say, "I can't." Encourage them to understand the difference between "I can't" and "This is hard for me."

• When you hear them protest their helplessness, try responding with something such as: "I know this is scary for you, and I know that you truly believe you can't do it. But I want you to know that I think you can succeed. It will be difficult, but I believe in your ability to accomplish this task."

• Be gentle and firm at the same time. While your gentleness communicates your compassion and warmth, your firmness communicates your belief in their strengths. Your affirmation also supports the intensity with which you want them to try. Neither gentleness nor firmness can be as effective alone as when you combine them.

Help your teenagers realize that being afraid to try something is never a good reason not to attempt it. Your children can develop their courage by trying difficult tasks while they have your immediate support and encouragement.

9. Practice letting go of your teenagers so they can develop greater trust in their strengths and abilities. Adolescence is a developmental stage normally marked by a gradual movement toward independence. Dependent young people resist this normal development because they lack self-confidence. They try to maintain their dependency to avoid the anxiety that independence brings them.

As a parent of dependent young people, you may have difficulty letting go because these adolescents present a dependent front and don't appear ready to assume more responsibility or freedom. Gradual letting go is the underlying principle in helping dependent teenagers. While encouraging your children to handle more autonomy, you must maintain

the amount and intensity of love and affection you offer
them. These teenagers may feel rejected if their greater freedom includes less contact with you. Freely express your
pride in and happiness about their growth and increasing
maturity. Your positive responses to their normal development assure them that they needn't equate their independence with rejection.

There are many ways to gradually increase your teenagers'
freedoms and responsibilities.

• With each birthday extend your dependent adolescents'
curfews. Reward their continuing responsible behavior with
expanded opportunities and freedoms.

• As your adolescents gain driving skills and experience,
gradually expand their freedom to drive more frequently
and increase their opportunities to use the car in a wider
variety of situations.

• With your children's progression through each grade
level, decrease your supervision of their academic performance. Remember, the grades they earn are theirs, not yours.
An important aspect of your adolescents' maturation is increasing responsibility for their school grades.

• Be less demanding and controlling about how your
teenagers keep their rooms. As a vital part of growing up,
teenagers must become increasingly responsible for their immediate environment. Though you may require minimal
standards because their rooms are part of the family home,
you must allow your young people to establish their personal standards. After all, these young people are growing
toward adulthood.

Dependent teenagers can handle progressive movements
toward increased freedom and responsibility far better than
sudden increases or no freedom at all. Letting go should be
a gradual process that both matches and encourages your
adolescents' maturation.

10. Encourage! Encourage! Encourage! Encouraging your dependent teenagers has been stressed throughout this section.
Because these young people possess minimal self-confidence,
they need your support and encouragement to meet the developmental challenges of adolescence.

Encourage them with your words. "We love having you as

part of our family." "It's really gratifying for me to see you developing into such a wonderful young lady."

Encourage their growth by giving them increased responsibility in the family. Assign them meaningful chores, and include them in important decision-making to reinforce their growth.

Maintain or even increase the amount of love, affection and attention you normally offer your dependent teenagers as they move toward independence. Remember to encourage their increased self-esteem by showing them respect. Your encouraging responses to your teenagers must be honest and come from your heart. Your actions express your good will, love and desire for your young people's success.

Dependency during adolescence can have several adaptive forms. The follower, admirer and imitator can serve positive functions in your family. But we must continue to help these young people develop greater internal strengths and higher self-esteem. The less healthy dependent teenagers, including the helpless, gullible and clinging vine, are in even greater need of our help. For these young people, dependency can become a permanent method to avoid the anxiety of social confrontation and leadership. With your encouragement and refusal to believe in their inadequacy, dependent young people can develop self-reliance and learn to use it effectively.

CHAPTER SEVEN

The Conforming Personality

Conforming teenagers are usually delightful. They seldom create disturbances and rarely have behavior problems. They actively seek to get along well with others and thrive in friendly, positive social environments. They're cooperative and try to support those around them. They care about others and want to help whenever they can. These young people are generous, selfless and willing to sacrifice for another's benefit. They strive for peaceful resolutions of conflict and feel most secure when their social relationships exhibit positive feelings and good will. These young people are the most affectionate of all personality types.

Conforming adolescents enjoy adherence to tradition. They like knowing the rules and social conventions so they can adapt comfortably by meeting expected standards. They feel most comfortable when they fulfill others' expectations of them.

The underlying purpose of conformity is to reduce the anxiety aroused by close contact with others and life's stresses. This social orientation seeks to reduce anxiety by assuring adolescents they're accepted and liked. Through their behavior, conforming teenagers say: "I feel good about myself and most comfortable when I know I'm meeting your expectations of me. When I please you, I assure myself that I can secure your acceptance and know that you like me."

The potential difficulty conforming adolescents encounter is sacrificing too much of themselves in an attempt to gain others' acceptance. If they reach the extreme of willingness to be whatever another person wants them to be, they lose sight of their own identity. This is extremely dangerous during adolescence when identity development is the main task of psychological development. Some teenagers so fear confrontation, disagreement and rejection they willingly sacrifice their own likes, preferences, opinions, thoughts and feelings for acceptance. When this social action continues too long, teenagers may experience identity panic and role diffusion. The role diffusion leaves them with no central identity, so they play out a collection of roles with different people in different situations. The identity panic can create anxiety and fear that may overwhelm young people when they realize they're drifting unpredictably between roles as a reaction to changing circumstances.

Conforming young people tend to be optimistic. They need a positive outlook on life to feel okay. This dynamic forces these teenagers to be enthusiastic and fun. However, their need for optimism may sometimes blind them to the real problems they should be struggling with. They'd rather avoid and deny unpleasant realities instead of confronting and resolving them.

"Time is a great healer."

"I'll be okay. I won't let it upset me."

"If I let things go, they always turn out all right."

Another potential problem for conforming adolescents is rigidity in their personality structure. When they cling too tightly to conformity and see everything positively, they lose their ability to be different. They forfeit the opportunity to stand up for what they think is right. They also sacrifice their chance to be original or creative. Their personalities become bland, their thoughts are impoverished, and they develop into boring individuals who have little originality, no uniqueness and few inherently interesting qualities.

▶ *Development of the Conforming Personality*

Adolescence is a development stage known for its conformity. Teenagers conform rigidly to peer group dress and hair styles. They adopt strict standards for their music, interests and activities. Conformity is one of the most powerful forces shaping their behavior.

Yet, for healthy, balanced development to continue, teenagers must also have the ability to be different. They must be assertive enough to risk conflict and rejection as they develop their own individuality. When they characteristically bend to most pressures to conform, they're probably best described by this chapter. To more fully understand conforming personalities, we need to understand what experiences have directed their development.

1. Parental modeling. Some parents value conformity, conflict avoidance and optimism as a preferred life pattern. They live out these values in their relationships and teach them to their children. Parental modeling is an especially powerful teaching tool because of the many opportunities parents have to reinforce kids' behavior. Parents may avoid conflict with unruly neighbors, decline returning defective store items they purchased or remain unrealistically optimistic when losing a job even though no new employment appears imminent. These parents may also tell their children to ignore the neighbor boy's selfishness, always "turn the other cheek" if attacked on the playground and never get discouraged.

2. Rigid homes. Households run on a tight schedule and regulated routine can influence children to order their lives accordingly. Young people who grow up in homes such as these learn to value order, routine and structure. They learn to be efficient and not get sidetracked by impulses. They maintain good behavioral control and can delay personal gratification for the good of the group or future benefit. As these children express their learned behaviors, their parents reinforce these values of order and routine.

"You certainly are developing good self-control."

"I like the way you're able to avoid fighting with the children across the street."

"You showed a lot of maturity by saying 'no' even though you really wanted to go with your friends."

3. Pressure to conform. Children are often heavily pressured to conform to older brothers' and sisters' power. Sometimes that pressure is subtle and loving.

"Bill, let's help Mom with the dishes. She's been working hard. It's the least we can do."

"I think it's selfish to not let your cousin play with your doll. Next time you should be more generous."

Other times the pressure to conform to an older sibling's wishes can be overt and difficult to defend against.

"If you tell Mom and Dad, I'll beat you up."

"I'm going to make sure every kid at school knows what a creep you are if you do that."

Some younger children learn their lesson too well. They learn life is much safer if they do only what pleases older or more powerful people. The pain of confrontation, disagreement, anger and rejection proves too much for them. They decide early in life to succumb through conformity to those around them.

4. Altered behavior. Some younger children simply learn that a happy way to be part of the family is to adapt to what's already happening in the family environment. If the family is sports-minded, the children may join soccer, tennis or Little League baseball. If their family chooses the outdoor life, they may learn to enjoy hiking, camping, fishing or three-wheeling. If born into a musical family, they may select their instrument and begin lessons early during elementary school. Excessively adaptive children often mature into conforming teenagers. They're comfortable only when they alter their behavior, adjust their expectations or delay their wants to please others.

5. Family conflict. Severe family conflict or parental separation and divorce are sometimes the root of adolescent conforming behavior. Belonging can be threatened by rejection or a breakup in the family. Children desperately need to belong. When the family unit's stability is challenged, their sense of belonging is severely shaken.

Certainly, severe parental fighting, physical violence, separation and divorce are major threats to children's security at home. But there are other threats too. When a parent travels frequently or is out of town for long time periods, young children experience inner disruption and anxiety. The same feelings occur when an older sibling leaves for college or the military. Even more trauma occurs when an older brother or sister is forced to leave home because parents can no longer tolerate or control the son's or daughter's behavior. Many times severe or long-term fighting between parents and older siblings causes younger children to adopt a conforming, "no waves" policy of dealing with parents.

6. Inadequate nurturing. Inadequate nurturing is sometimes part of conforming teenagers' developmental history. Perhaps their parents were raised in relatively non-nurturing homes and couldn't teach their children how to feel or express physical and emotional affection. Maybe these significant adults have been too hurt or too frustrated to freely demonstrate softer, more vulnerable feelings. Whatever the cause, many children who grow up without adequate affection experience difficulty developing healthy identities during adolescence.

Some teenagers see conformity as a way to get close to others. "If I can be like them, maybe they'll like and accept me." For these young people conformity represents an attempt to gain intimacy and identity at the same time. Of course, results of this effort can't be positive or long-lasting. True intimacy can exist only when both people have fairly well-developed identities.

7. Excessive nurturing. Excessive and possessive nurturing, which tends to retard children's emotional growth, can facilitate the development of a conforming personality. This kind of parental attention is usually quite controlling and often passive-aggressive in its orientation. The passive-aggressive style of parenting is illustrated when parents characteristically withhold their child from participation in activities outside the home. Their not allowing the child to participate carries an element of rejection simply by not being involved.

Overprotection is a common form of parental attention that communicates the parents' distrust of their children's abilities and skills.

"Mommy can't let you ride your bike. You might get hurt."

"I don't want you to play with those children. They're too mean."

Children inaccurately learn that they are inadequate and must stay under their parents' protective care. As they grow older, they learn to fear separation from their parents and seek to remedy that situation by becoming whatever types of people the parents want them to be. The same dynamic is transferred to other adults and peers whose opinions may dictate conforming behavior to these teenagers.

8. Criticism. Some parents and other adults criticize children who express their individuality. They're threatened by young people who intensely state their feelings. They misinterpret their determination as stubbornness. These adults forget children aren't experienced in their social skills, and that they sometimes simply overstate their assertiveness because they lack experience. Reacting to these children in a strong, punitive manner is inappropriate and may discourage further expressions of their feelings and opinions. During therapy sessions some conforming teenagers can recall specific frightening episodes of adults harshly punishing them for expressing their individuality. Some vividly remember the exact incident that prompted their decision to conform to others' expectations rather than risk further assertions of their own identities.

9. Peer groups. Peer groups have a powerful force on their members to conform to their specific standards. Peer pressure heavily influences clothing fashions and hair styles; selection of friends, music and cars; choice of classes and churches; gestures, facial expressions, behavior, language and academic achievement levels. Though virtually all teenagers are impacted by peer pressure, some are far less capable of resisting than others, even when such resistance is desirable. Some adolescents find it intolerable to resist their peers' expectations. Their anxieties about rejection, being alone and alienation prevent them from differing in any significant way from their peer group members.

10. Church teachings. Some churches' teachings heavily influence and reinforce adolescents' conforming behavior. Young people are taught to avoid conforming to the world. "Do not conform any longer to the pattern of this world, but be transformed by the renewing of your mind. Then you will be able to test and approve what God's will is—his good, pleasing and perfect will" (Romans 12:2).

The admonition not to conform to the world's standards is well-taken. However, problems arise when teenagers are taught to conform to everything the minister preaches, the church youth leader says and the Sunday school teacher teaches. The scripture says we're to be "transformed by the renewing of (our) mind," not conformed. Conforming is much shallower than being transformed and renewed. Conforming is something people do by an act of will. The Holy Spirit generates being transformed and renewed; it's already happening. People's choice in transformation is whether they'll acknowledge the Spirit's influence in their lives.

Parents should be sensitive to new Christians' tendency to overidentify with the church's or church youth group's standards and beliefs. Teenagers do this to ensure approval and acceptance. New group members often appear extremely "spiritual." Their religious language, regular Bible study, daily devotions, intense prayers, Bible memorization, and faith sharing may be motivated by their need for acceptance as much as by their love for Christ. The same religious activities may display deep spiritual growth or express a need for acceptance; or in some cases these activities may indicate both.

11. It works. Teenagers use the conforming social orientation because it works. As it significantly reduces young people's anxiety, they use it again and again.

▶ Healthy Forms of the Conforming Personality

The conforming personality tends to be a sociable individual. These young people know how to make their defensive orientations work for them. They typically get along well with others. It's easy to spot healthy examples of this social orientation. You may have one in your family. Following are two examples of healthy, adaptive forms of the conforming personality.

The Counselor. Seventeen-year-old William is a good example of a healthy, productive form of the conforming adolescent personality. As a high school senior, he volunteered for a church peer counseling class. Because of his apparent maturity, he was one of only five high school young people allowed to participate; the rest of the class were adults. As the 13-week training period progressed, he discovered a lot about himself and told these discoveries to the class.

William was the oldest of four children. His dad was a career Navy man who had served sea duty during much of William's childhood and adolescence. As the oldest child with a continually absent father, William voluntarily took on many responsibilities to help his mother. Because he was especially kind and patient with his younger brother and sisters, his mother often requested his help with the other children while she shopped, cooked, cleaned house or ran errands. Usually he happily complied. He became adept at helping them solve their problems and creative in discovering ways to resolve their conflicts. Recognizing his efforts, the younger children usually responded well to his attempts to calm them after getting hurt or when feeling sick.

When William was 13, his youngest sister, 9 years old, suddenly contracted meningitis and died in two weeks. His father couldn't get home until a week after her death. During her illness and the week following her death, William was a major source of support for the rest of the family. Fortunately, there were several friends from their church who drew close during those difficult weeks. William accepted their support and compassion and was also able to give of himself to his mother, brother and sister.

Because he spent so much time helping his mother and assisting his younger siblings, William socialized little with friends his age. He felt uncomfortable at school because he was uncertain how to act. Unstructured times, particularly lunch, were difficult for him. He wasn't so ill-at-ease in his church youth group, but he still felt somewhat awkward.

William's solution to his social uneasiness was to be as kind and helpful as he could. He believed if he were thoughtful, helpful and cheerful, others would always like and appreciate him. At home, church and school, William sought to please everyone. He was so comfortable and easy to be around that many of his friends sought him out when they needed to vent their frustrations. His attentive listening, genuine concern, patience and helpful suggestions gained him a reputation for being a good friend to talk with about problems.

William wasn't aware of the motivation that caused him to develop these constructive, helpful personality traits. He didn't realize his social orientation was helping him as much as it was serving others. Counseling became his way of making social contact with his peers. This role gave him enough structure to feel secure with others. Being gentle and encouraging enabled him to make the only social contact comfortable for him. Because he was friendly and supportive, he could almost completely avoid harshness, conflict and confrontation with his peers and adults. His optimism was also a useful, appropriate response. Being optimistic when helping others enabled him to deny his personal pain and avoid problems in his own life.

William styled himself as a peacemaker. He consciously sought to model his life after Matthew 5:9, "Blessed are the peacemakers, for they will be called sons of God."

The Greeter. Arriving to address an urban church youth group, the guest speaker met 16-year-old Samantha at the door. She greeted him with a bright, friendly smile, sparkling eyes and a bubbly: "Hi! How are you? We're so glad you can be with us tonight. I'm Samantha. I'm looking forward to hearing what you have to say. Let me introduce you to our youth minister." From then until 15 minutes into the program, Samantha stood at the door, greeting people as they arrived. She welcomed everyone and spent more time with first-time visitors and new members, making sure they were introduced to others in the group. She was marvelous! What a blessing to have someone like her to help people feel comfortable and welcome the minute they walk through the door!

After the meeting the speaker and youth pastor went out for dessert. They talked about Samantha. Her youth pastor related that Samantha always acted like she did that evening. At virtually every youth meeting, Bible study and social event, she happily assumed the position of greeter and welcomed people. She'd never been appointed to that position nor had anyone ever asked her to do it. But her youth pastor remembered she'd started welcoming people within a few short weeks after her graduation into the high school group.

When not fulfilling her self-appointed role as greeter, Samantha was rather quiet. She was always there and obviously interested in what happened, but she wasn't actively involved. She was a great listener but volunteered few comments in group discussions or even casual conversations among her friends. She felt most comfortable with others when she was in the greeter role. That's when she felt the personal freedom to interact and be spontaneous with others. Her personal history and family background helps us understand how Samantha developed her conforming interpersonal orientation.

She was the fourth of five children. Her mother and father were extremely different from each other. Dad was a free spirit, uninhibited who wanted to live for today. Mom was exceptionally conscientious, conservative and believed in living rationally and cautiously to guarantee the future as much as possible. Their marriage seemed destined to end, and it did.

When Samantha was 5 years old, her parents divorced. She and her four brothers and sisters lived with their mother. They seldom saw their dad after the divorce. He never played a major role in supporting the family, nor did he participate in the children's care. Her mother dated other men only a few times but never remarried. She didn't trust men and felt more in control by being single.

Samantha never dealt with the psychological pain caused by her parents' divorce. She never talked with anyone about her feelings of loss and sadness. Her mom became protective of her children, carefully monitoring their activities and choices of friends. She also supervised their bedtimes, homework schedules and household chores, while making sure they ate well and wore proper clothing. Observing her mother, Samantha learned that life and relationships were fragile, and much care had to be taken to protect and pre-serve both.

Samantha also learned not to get too involved with friends. She found she could be liked and accepted when she gave people what made them feel good. When she smiled, others smiled back. When she talked in a friendly manner, most people reacted with friendly responses. She also learned that when these shallow relationships broke up, there was less pain than when deep friendships ended.

Becoming a greeter suited Samantha's needs. It allowed her to make contact with large numbers of her peers and adults, and she could use her limited social skills to their maximum benefit. By smiling and being friendly, she elicited the same responses from others. An additional benefit to her greeter role was her lack of time to enter into deeper rela-tionships, even though she did facilitate her friends' relation-ships with one another. She remained cheery and positive and was happy to have the sense of belonging and relation-ship she had.

▶ Unhealthy Forms of the Conforming Personality

Each of the personality orientations in this book have both healthy and unhealthy forms. Teenagers are seldom completely described by only one personality type. Most people have elements of two or more orientations in their personalities. They also usually possess both adaptive and maladaptive characteristics of their particular orientations.

Conformity becomes unhealthy when young people feel they can't confront others or when development of their in-dividual differences is severely hampered. Conforming then becomes a prison confining teenagers to a narrow range of social behaviors thought to be safe and acceptable. When this limiting occurs, young people's quality of life and fulfill-ment level are seriously limited. Now we'll meet two un-healthy forms of this defensive structure.

The Yes-Man. At age 18, Solomon went to see his guidance counselor at the community college he attended. At the be-ginning of his second year, he had no idea what career path he wanted to follow. As he entered the counselor's office, he was extremely nervous, not knowing what was expected of him or how to proceed. But as soon as the counselor initiated the conversation and asked pertinent questions, Solomon relaxed and felt more secure. He answered the inquiries as accurately as he could and tried to assist his counselor's efforts to guide him. His personal history and family background helped the counselor understand why finding his career orientation was so difficult for him.

Solomon was the younger of two boys in his family. Both parents were disciplinarians but operated differently. His father was firm and at times harsh in his demands. He posted household rules on the kitchen door and insisted both boys obey them. He handled all infractions quickly through spankings, restrictions or loss of privileges, in addition to intense, lengthy verbal tirades.

Solomon's mother also expected strict obedience of rules; however, her discipline and disapproval were more subtle. She demanded that her boys respect all authority, especially their parents'. She based her life on the premise, "It's always best to follow rules, to fulfill what's expected and get along with others, no matter what the personal cost." When Solomon and his brother disobeyed, she disciplined primarily by withdrawing her affection. She became silent, looked disapprovingly at them, stiffened her neck, slowly shook her head from side to side and walked out of the room. The only avenue back into her favor was through apologies, admissions of guilt, promises it would never happen again and many requests for her forgiveness. She made it clear that any forgiveness she offered was neither deserved nor warranted by either of the boys.

Both parents' punishment methods carried messages of rejection and separation. Both discipline approaches suggested that misbehavior made the boys unacceptable and unlovable. The only way to be okay again was to subjugate themselves completely to their parents' conditions and perceptions. They had to reject any sense of individuality, differences and dignity to again be acceptable for a friendly relationship with either parent.

In addition to this atmosphere of harsh discipline, it was

even more difficult for Solomon to develop adaptive behavior because of his home life's instability. His family moved every two years because of his father's employment searches. A semiskilled laborer, his father had difficulty keeping a job for long. He usually began experiencing conflict with his supervisors within the first year and then was either fired or quit his job sometime during the next year. Solomon's childhood was a long series of changes in schools, neighborhoods and friends. He learned to meet new people but never developed any long-term relationships.

In junior high he experienced a series of heavy, painful rejections. One of his most traumatic experiences occurred near the end of seventh grade, shortly after his family had moved to yet another new city. Within a few weeks after starting school, he became infatuated with a girl in his humanities class. He knew he'd have to make his move soon because school would be over in less than a month. So he risked asking her to go to a movie with him. She smiled; then her smile broke into laughter. To intensify the situation, she then told some eighth-grade boys who were her friends. For the rest of the school year, they ridiculed and made fun of him. He imagined it was because of his accent and different clothing styles. But this rejection and intimidation intensified his feeling painfully odd and out of place.

Solomon's guidance counselor realized this young man's problems went much deeper than his reported difficulty choosing a career. He exhibited an extreme fear of rejection. He was terribly hesitant to develop relationships, fearing he'd lose them. He was extremely self-conscious and sensitive to any differences he perceived between himself and others. He dared not strongly state his opinions or attitudes and would never consider openly disagreeing with anyone. He felt most comfortable when he was in a structured social situation in which there were rules to observe and clear expectations to follow. He readily did what teachers and others told him to do; and in group discussions he openly agreed with the points made and others' opinions, rather than tell his own.

Solomon couldn't tolerate his own negative feelings; they were too threatening. Dislike for someone, disagreement with what was being said, anger about what was being done and unhappiness with part of his life gave him terrible anxiety. He'd quickly repress these impulses and consciously deny them. They threatened his tenuous sense of security in his relationships with people. Solomon couldn't tolerate any indication that he might be different from others. External indicators such as dressing differently or internal signals such as feeling angry at someone frightened him terribly. He forced himself into perpetual optimism and positive thinking to guard against the threat of any negative thoughts or feelings.

The Chameleon. This is probably the least healthy form of the conforming personality orientation. The chameleon is similar to both the imitator, a form of the dependent orientation, and the yes-man. The primary difference is the level of consciousness individuals have while defending themselves. Both the yes-man and the imitator are aware of what they're doing. The yes-man consciously decides to protect himself or herself from rejection. The imitator chooses to imitate those he or she respects in order to vicariously experience the same respect and admiration he or she has for others. Chameleons, however, operate their defenses almost completely without conscious awareness. Psychologists would consider these conforming teenagers to be more primitive or less psychologically sophisticated. The less conscious people are of their defenses, the more likely it is that intense pain or trauma occurred earlier in their lives.

Gina was 16 years old before she saw a professional therapist. She came first with her mother and half sister and then saw the therapist several months alone. Later, she joined her mother, half sister and stepfather in family counseling sessions. The events that led to her therapy encompassed most of her life; they are typical of the trauma level that usually causes self-damaging and rigid personality orientations.

When Gina was 3 years old, her parents divorced. Her father moved out of state, and she had few memories of him. During the next few years her mother had two live-in boyfriends. The first man offered Gina some parenting, but was primarily involved with her mother. After Gina's half sister was born two years later, the couple's relationship deteriorated and he left. When the second boyfriend came to live with her family, he was also involved with Gina's mother. However, after a short time his interest turned to Gina too. Before her mother had broken off her relationship with this second boyfriend, he had sexually molested Gina three times. Frightened and confused, Gina didn't know what to do about the genital fondling she'd experienced. She never told anyone, including her mother, because the man had threatened to beat her if she did.

When Gina was 7 years old, her mother remarried. Everything progressed well the first year; then life caved in on Gina. One evening while her mother was bowling on her league night, her stepfather came into her room and lay beside her on her bed. He forced her to manually stimulate him while he did the same to her. He said nothing until he got up to leave her room. "You better not say anything that would hurt your mother, or you won't live through it!" Gina was frightened, hurt, angry and thoroughly confused. Memories of her earlier molestations overwhelmed her. It was happening again. And she didn't know how to stop it.

Her stepfather continued this sexual harassment, molesting her as often as three times a week. After several months he increased his demands to oral stimulation, and within a year he was regularly having intercourse with her. She was terrified he'd hurt her, and she was even more fearful that her mother might find out.

Gina was also angry that her mother had never discovered their "secret." "Wasn't it obvious? How could she live here and not know?" Gina lived with this confusion, plus dread, anger and guilt. She dreaded being alone with her stepfather. She avoided him whenever she could, but he'd have sex with her in the house, car or wherever he could get her alone. She was angry at him, and she was also angry at her mother. She was caught in a position where she couldn't keep from betraying someone she loved. By keeping the secret, she'd already betrayed her mother; and if she told, she'd betray her stepfather.

One Saturday morning when she was 14, her stepfather told her this would be the last time he'd have sex with her because he was afraid she might get pregnant. She felt great relief, but also experienced rejection and betrayal. In a few days he approached Gina's half sister. Several years before, she'd figured out what was happening between Gina and their stepfather and vowed never to let it happen to her. After the second time he made advances to her, she told her mother, who called the Child Protective Service. The police investigated, removed the stepfather from the home and initiated counseling for the entire family.

When Gina was in therapy, she became involved with a nearby church that had an active high school youth ministry. She felt safe there and attended regularly. As she participated more, the severity of her social impairment resulting from her trauma became increasingly apparent. When she was with a group of girlfriends, she became giggly, happy and fun, just like they were. When she was with a group of boys, she was boisterously loud and mischievous, just like they were. And when she was with an adult group she was thoughtful and pensive, modeling the behavior she saw around her. Unconsciously she assumed the characteristics of the people she associated with. When asked about her behavior, she said she had no idea she was acting this way.

The counselor clearly understood Gina's situation. The vast majority of Gina's elementary school and early adolescent years had been overshadowed by her ongoing trauma. The impact of her sexual abuse had affected virtually every area of her life. She felt embarrassed and ashamed around other girls, fearing they could sense what she'd been doing. She also felt intensely uncomfortable and guarded around men and boys. Because of her past experiences, she mistook any interest from them to be sexual and realized that was the only way she knew to relate to men and boys.

Gina had repressed, controlled and denied her emotions and impulses for so many years she often couldn't even recognize what was going on inside her. To survive those six years in her incestuous home life, she'd psychologically anesthetized herself to her thoughts and emotions. Now, she couldn't regain her lost self-awareness. Increasing her consciousness level became one of her therapy's major goals.

Gina had essentially lost herself. Since she had so little

control of what was happening to her, she lost her sense of individuality and had yet to begin developing her identity. Her only way of relating was to automatically become like the people she was with at the time.

► Effects of Conforming Behavior on Others

The purpose of conforming behavior is to avoid any confrontation and diminish interpersonal differences to facilitate comfortable social relationships. Therefore, we would expect the major effect of this personality orientation to be positive. And as long as a teenager doesn't become extreme or rigid in his or her use of conformity, this young person has positive experiences with others.

Most teenagers and adults like to associate with conforming adolescents. This personality type makes others feel comfortable and relaxed. The conforming adolescent makes sure conversations are light and pleasant; he or she says only nice things or compliments others to make them feel good. This type of adolescent often expresses tender, warm and caring feelings to illustrate his or her support, care and respect for others. William, the "counselor," offers us a good example of how this type of teenager can offer others genuine, helpful care. A conforming adolescent knows that when you show others appreciation, value and acceptance, they'll respond cheerfully and positively. This personality type exemplifies that smiling at someone usually draws a smile in return.

Another common effect of being with a conforming teenager is feeling happy. Everything looks better and we feel more hopeful when we're around an individual who has positive perceptions and cheerful responses to life itself. However, if this optimism is too unrealistic, it can be irritating. Remember, for this type of young person, optimism is a defense against personal pain or discomfort. Sometimes he or she carries that positive outlook to an extreme and loses the ability to respond appropriately and meaningfully to worries and concerns. In parenting one of these young people, you may experience irritation or aggravation and not feel heard as a response to his or her extreme optimism.

Another negative reaction you may have to conformity is frustration. Since this personality orientation adapts so readily to current rules, expectations and needs of others, it's difficult to know who this young person really is. The need for comfort and ease in relationships creates a major block to any deeper self-disclosure and intimacy development with others. Risking our feelings is serious for each of us, but especially for a conforming teenager. Fear that others won't like or respect something he or she values is too overwhelming.

After frustration you may experience boredom with a conforming adolescent. Inability to get past his or her rigid defenses leaves only limited opportunities for personal interaction. This young person's lack of creativity and spontaneity gives you a bland feeling. A conforming teenager doesn't offer much fun or excitement; he or she is just nice.

Power-oriented people sometimes take advantage of this teenager's conformity in much the same way they use other teenagers' dependency. To get along and avoid conflict with others, a conforming adolescent allows himself or herself to be used by these strong personality types.

► Guidelines for Parenting Conforming Adolescents

The teenagers in this chapter make parenting seem pretty easy. Since they rarely rebel, if at all, their presence in the family doesn't strain relationships like other adolescent types do. When there's no turmoil surrounding your adolescent children, you may be tempted to "let well enough alone." Unfortunately, a lack of problems can indicate inappropriate and unhealthy adolescent growth or development. If you lack any tension or stress during your children's adolescent years, look for arrested personality development or passive behavior. An almost complete lack of turmoil or problems during adolescence may indicate the presence of conforming personalities.

After reading this chapter, you may conclude that your teenagers are primarily conforming personalities. The following guidelines should help both you and your adolescents work to meet their needs.

1. "Listen" carefully to the meanings your teenagers' behaviors express. You know your adolescent children better than anyone. Their gestures, facial expressions, postures, behavior patterns and special words contain certain meanings. Their past histories and experiences usually shape their behavior patterns in unique ways. Teenagers' current actions often express much of how they feel about themselves and others and how they perceive the world they live in.

You dare not assume you understand your teenagers' motivations or meanings expressed through their behavior. Recognize that they can surprise you. Even though you may formulate your own thoughts about what they're doing, check with them to find out if your perceptions are accurate. Sometimes they may be unsure of why they act the way they do. But you can still learn something from their responses.

"When you stay in your room instead of eating dinner with us, it usually means you're upset about something. Is something happening that we can talk about?"

"You certainly seem bubbly and cheerful this afternoon. Did something special happen at school today?"

Finding specific meaning for conforming teenagers' behavior is particularly difficult because in a sense their behavior doesn't belong to them. They've imitated or borrowed it from someone else, and therein lies its primary meaning for them. Seek to understand why your adolescents need to conform so strongly to others.

2. Continually reassure your teenagers of their importance to your family. Teenagers need to know they're valued family members. Conforming adolescents are excessively sensitive about their acceptance and belonging. They need constant assurance that they're valued and have an important place in your home. Encourage them, and let them know they'd be greatly missed if they weren't there.

Belonging is important for most adolescents. Conforming teenagers are especially concerned about fitting in. They seek to be like others in their attempts to be accepted. They're afraid that any significant difference will lead to their rejection. You can help your teenagers actively gain value as a family member while they grow in their abilities to express their individuality.

Try to surprise your conforming adolescents with statements that indicate their value when they've done nothing to earn your admiration. "I like having you as part of our family." "You know, things wouldn't be the same around here without you." "Do you have any idea how much you'd be missed if you weren't here?" Mix in bear hugs, a few warm nudges and some friendly pokes and pats to help them believe you really do mean what you say. Periodically you might write your assurances in a note or on a special card and put it in their lunch sack or tape it onto their mirror.

Another way to help your conforming teenagers feel secure is by making sure they fulfill some significant household roles. Let them do chores that make a difference in the family's smooth functioning. Cooking, doing laundry, ironing, dusting, vacuuming, shopping, doing dishes, lawn-mowing and being responsible for regular errands are meaningful tasks teenagers can assume. Reinforce and affirm their efforts when they fulfill their responsibilities. In addition, let them see the disadvantages others in the family experience when they don't carry out their duties. Take care not to manipulate your children's behavior through guilt.

Recognize the importance of belonging for your conforming teenagers, and help them feel secure and important as part of your family. With this kind of support you can help these young people fulfill some of their deepest needs.

3. Reinforce your teenagers' expressions of their individuality and uniqueness. Conforming young people experience great apprehension about being different from others. Even positive differences threaten them. Sometimes they'll purposefully do poorly on an exam, intentionally come in second in a race or quietly decline an opportunity to tell a party joke rather than call attention to their special skills or talents. These teenagers take peer-group conformity to the extreme. Not conforming lowers their defenses and seriously threatens their identity's development.

As a parent, you're in a strategic position to help your conforming teenagers. Use your relationship to help them develop a personal identity. Since conforming teenagers struggle with being different, tell them how much you enjoy their unique qualities.

Think about those special characteristics, habits and modes of expression that make your adolescents one of a kind.

- What things about your children do you especially like?
- What makes you enjoy having them around?
- When they're gone for a time, what do you miss about them?

Think about your teenagers' communication styles and decide what seems special about each one.

- Do they have a unique sense of humor?
- What about their ability with words? Can they choose just the right word at the right time?
- What about the uncanny way they express their thoughts and feelings with accuracy and insight?

Consider your children's physical appearance. Is there something about them that you think is especially neat?

- What do you notice about their hair? their eyes?
- Which facial expression or gesture seems unique to them?
- What about the way they walk or their body movements?

Tell them you think they have something special about them that sets them apart from others. Conforming teenagers value their individuality; yet they're also frightened by it. Your parental encouragement and reinforcement of their uniqueness can strongly influence their identity formation.

4. Encourage your teenagers to express their thoughts and feelings. Conforming adolescents are afraid to be different from their peers because they might be rejected. Because of their apprehension, these young people often withhold their attitudes, opinions and feelings from others. By not volunteering how they think and feel, they protect themselves from the rejection and isolation they fear. Their insecurity and self-doubt often build as these teenagers suppress their insights, perceptiveness and individual attitudes.

Your conforming teenagers need you to help them identify and express their thoughts and opinions. You may provide the extra push your conforming young people need to get them over their hurdle of fear. Accept and reinforce their thinking. Provide opportunities for your children to express themselves with minimal risk. Establish regular family meetings to discuss vacation plans, chore assignments, weekend activities and so on. These meetings offer an excellent nonthreatening environment for your teenagers to say what they really think.

Be willing to search for your young people's thoughts. Assure them you want to know what's going on inside their head and heart. Be tenacious, but not pushy. Develop the art of probing, but not so forcefully your children back away. Be persistent, and your patience may be rewarded. When there's something especially important to discuss, find a way to be alone with your teenager. Go for a ride in the car, or take a walk together. Go out for a hamburger or go shopping. Do something enjoyable that allows time for talking about thoughts and feelings.

Tell your young people you find their thoughts interesting. Don't be threatened by what they think. All of us experience thoughts and feelings we'd never act on. Teenagers need to think through their full range of options. They need time to mentally work out the possible consequences of their various actions. The more comfortable they feel talking these things over with you, the more you can help them. Accept and encourage their openness instead of judging and correcting their ideas. "That's an approach I never thought of. Tell me more about how that might work." This kind of support is more accepting than: "That idea has already been tried. It never works."

Conforming teenagers hesitate to express their thoughts, attitudes and opinions. Their fears of rejection cause them to suppress any individualistic thinking. As their parent, you can help them develop confidence as they explore their thinking abilities.

5. Encourage your teenagers' creativity. Creativity suggests doing something differently, a frightening and threatening concept for conforming adolescents. This personality type fights all creative freedom because of their fears of rejection if others see them as different. By encouraging their originality, you actually support your children's healthy identity development. The supportive family in the home is perhaps the safest environment for these young people to explore their creativity. These young people need a non-judgmental atmosphere in which they know they're safe from being laughed at or thought of as stupid. This supportive atmosphere is vital for conforming teenagers' continued growth toward mature identity development.

Involve your teenagers in brainstorming sessions in which all ideas are considered and enjoyed. Brainstorming demands two things: No one can make fun of any idea and no one can ridicule anyone who suggests an idea. Families can enjoy these sessions. Individuals can offer a wide range of silly as well as serious ideas, fun as well as serious considerations. When your family has experienced the fun and value of these creative sessions, give your adolescents actual household tasks requiring their creative thoughts and actions. Let them rearrange the garage storage area, the tool shed or their closet. Let them design your family Christmas letter's art work or have them create a custom Christmas card. Perhaps they could construct a unique address-marker for the front of your house. Maybe there's a small section of your yard where they could landscape and maintain the plants on their own. The possibilities are endless, limited only by your creativity.

Conforming personalities resist their creativity because they fear rejection because of their uniqueness. You can provide a safe environment in your home where creative thoughts and actions are stimulated and reinforced.

6. Encourage your teenagers to be spontaneous. Spontaneity is important to teenagers' psychological health. It helps them express their full range of emotions and enhances their capacities for creativity. It helps them communicate their real thoughts, attitudes and feelings to those around them. Personal spontaneous expressions help teenagers develop their self-concepts.

Conforming adolescents fear spontaneity the same way they fear creativity. For them, spontaneous actions present dangers such as being different, standing out in the crowd and getting attention. These teenagers need to control their words and actions and seal off their spontaneous reactions before others recognize them.

Conforming young people need your help to develop spontaneity. Home is often the safest place for them to try their varied forms of self-expression. You can supply encouragement, suggestions and, most important, acceptance of your teenagers as they experiment with spontaneous self-expression. You can protect your young people from ridicule and derision as they seek freedom from their overcontrolling defenses. The following ideas may stimulate your own strategies for helping your teenagers.

• Use material from TV programs, movies, songs and books to elicit spontaneous expressions from your conforming teenagers. For example, when you're watching television together, ask your young people for their reactions to particular scenes—both dramatic and comedic. Make your request offhand and non-imposing.

"I can't believe he did that! Did you see it coming? What did you think of that?"

"This has to be the funniest show on television! I love her sense of humor. What part did you like best?"

• Encourage your conforming teenagers to outwardly express their inner reactions to events around them. When you hear the loud screech of screaming brakes, you might ask, "What's the first thing you think of when you hear that sound?"

• In situations that typically elicit strong emotions, check with your teenagers to see how they're feeling. Let them see and hear how the same situation affects you. Help them understand that spontaneous emotional responses are normal and healthy. When they do risk telling their spontaneous feelings and thoughts, assure them that they're okay. They need to know right away that you don't think less of them because of their spontaneous reactions.

Conforming adolescents lack a normal capacity for spontaneous reactions. They need and can benefit from your encouragement and reinforcement of their efforts to develop more spontaneous freedom.

7. Help your teenagers know it's okay to have and express negative feelings. Conforming young people are apprehensive about anger, depression, resentment and other negative feelings because they're afraid something is wrong with them. They fear expressing their negative feelings because they don't want others to think badly of them or reject them. We must help our teenagers learn to deal with their negative emotions, even though their struggle won't be pleasant to experience. Allow them to express themselves at home. Help them discover appropriate ways to release their feelings and impulses.

When your conforming teenagers are upset with family members, encourage them to express their anger. Then talk with them about their feelings until the intensity is gone. This process helps conforming adolescents build confidence in their abilities to handle feelings successfully. It also helps them realize that intense, painful emotions are usually temporary.

Model healthy expressions of your negative emotions. Let your teenagers hear you raise your voice. Let them see your tears. Your transparency shows them how it's done. It also helps them understand that horrible things don't have to happen just because we sometimes feel bad.

Conforming teenagers need encouragement, reassurance and examples to follow to feel more comfortable expressing their own negative emotions. You can make a big difference by helping your young people develop healthy ways to handle their emotions.

8. Encourage and support your teenagers' attempts to rebel. This suggestion makes no sense to most other adolescent types' parents. But conforming teenagers find it difficult to actively push against anyone. In their minds, rebellion seems dangerous and foolish. Rebellion would bring the thing they fear most—separation and alienation from others. They're also afraid that if they start rebelling, they may not be able to control their aggressive impulses.

Conforming young people need your support and reassurance. They need to know you will not reject or severely punish them when they do exhibit rebellious behavior. They need reassurance that you will help them control their rebellious impulses.

Try to recognize their subtle expressions of rebellion. These teenagers are cautious and wary when they start rebelling. They "test the waters" of your response before diving into full adolescent rebelliousness. Show acceptance and genuine concern for their well-being during their initial ventures into rebellion.

Allow and encourage your young people to express differences of opinion. They may find it easier to discuss their differences before they act on them. Accept what they say as valid for them. This doesn't mean you have to agree with their position. If you agree, there won't be any differences or rebellion. So let the difference in opinions remain. Discuss the issue with them, and say something like: "Well, I guess we disagree about this. But then we're two different people, and we're not going to agree about everything, are we? Maybe we can agree to disagree on some things, and go on loving and accepting each other." This kind of statement helps them learn that differences among people are important. Your response also reaffirms your continued acceptance and models your willingness to listen to other opinions.

When you're the parent of conforming adolescents, encourage not only verbal differences, but allow your children to act differently. This position is tough. This is where your insecurity begins to show. This is where you have to trust your teenagers' abilities to handle more responsibility for their lives. This means letting go while they grow up. Don't wait until they're adults; it's too late then.

When their rebellious expressions produce too much trauma, disrupt the household or stimulate disrespect of others, you must put limits on what behavior is and isn't acceptable to you. Clarify your standard that while rebellion is necessary and allowable, disrespect and violence aren't. Be careful not to overreact. Overreaction has two possible responses: You may push your teenagers back into extreme conformity, or you may push them into more extreme forms of rebellion. Your task is to be encouraging and supportive while providing security through safe limits.

9. Help your teenagers learn to graciously receive good things. Most conforming teenagers feel uncomfortable receiving from others. They enjoy giving because it confirms their goodness, kindness and generosity, but receiving leaves them vulnerable. When these young people receive from others, they aren't doing anything to affirm their personal value and okayness. When they receive with no opportunity to give in return, they feel insecure. As a parent, you can help your conforming teenagers become good receivers and generous givers.

Arrange opportunities for your teenagers to receive from others. Birthday parties and other special events focused on your teenager offer the easiest possibilities. Observe how your adolescents respond at parties given in their honor. Are they embarrassed? low-key and cool? excited? Discuss their responses later. Encourage them to express how they felt about the experience. Gently tell them what you observed.

You may express your love and caring for your children by giving to them many ways. Things like money, clothes, sports equipment, school supplies, stereos and cars are typical gifts for special occasions. But don't forget your gifts of time and energy in preparing meals, running a taxi service, helping with homework, listening to problems and counseling on what to do with painful friendships. These are some of the most valuable gifts you can give your adolescents. Your continued giving helps them gradually feel more comfortable as a receiver.

You can also teach your conforming teenagers how to receive gifts from people. The art of gracious receiving is a social skill that people must learn. No one is born with it. Tell them you realize that receiving can be an uncomfortable experience. Discuss their feelings with them. Tell them how you and some of your friends handle those kinds of situations. If they're willing, role play receiving situations with them. Be sure to talk about their experiences. Encourage them to tell how they felt and discuss the new skills they learned.

Receiving from others makes conforming adolescents extremely uncomfortable. You can help your teenagers learn to handle these difficult experiences.

Conforming adolescents can be delightfully healthy young people who relate well socially and build positive self-concepts. But they can also be relatively unhealthy individuals who have severely disturbed relationship patterns. Parents can offer valuable help. After reading this chapter you've learned some specific ways you can help these young people become increasingly adaptive in their personality orientation.

CHAPTER EIGHT

The Responsible Personality

This personality type is as close to the social ideal as adolescents can get. These young people are typically successful, well-liked, respected and happy. They represent a blend of power-oriented and conforming personalities. They possess both leadership and friendship capabilities, follow through with commitments and respect authority.

Parents are happy to have responsible teenagers. These young people are mature, handle themselves comfortably in social situations and impress others with their strength and self-confidence. They reflect good, logical reasoning and fair-mindedness. In addition, they maintain a capacity for compassion, sensitivity and a desire to help others.

Responsible teenagers appear to have few problems. They feel most confident and comfortable when they control their lives and operate in warm, pleasant social relationships. Responsible teenagers impress others with their inner strengths and caring attitudes, while reinforcing those same characteristics in their behavior.

Responsible young people fear defeat and failure. They strive to avoid rejection and isolation. Generally, they don't like confrontation, so they seek positive, happy relationships. They motivate themselves to be helpful, caring and supportive in their social contacts so others respond and affirm them as good citizens. Responsible teenagers' behavior essentially says, "I'm comfortable when I control my life, exercise strength and leadership and when I'm warm and supportive in my social relationships." This personality type has many advantages. But when these teenagers rigidly uphold their responsibilities or express them in extreme forms, negative results can occur.

▶ Development of the Responsible Personality

Responsible teenagers often appear to be mature young people with no personal problems. But we must remember that all social orientations attempt to diminish the anxiety of interacting with others and dealing with life's stresses. To understand why teenagers act the way they do, we need to know what's happened to them in their past. Knowledge of significant events and people impacting them earlier in their lives gives us valuable insight into how we can best help and live with these young people. Several factors in these teenagers' personal histories contribute to the development of their responsible personalities.

1. High energy level. Most responsible teenagers are active and energetic. This personality orientation requires a healthy body and at least an average metabolism level. These young people usually involve themselves in many different activities. They're often leaders in school clubs, athletics and student governments. Frequently, they also participate in their churches and church youth groups. Good academic performance, an active social life, involvement in family activities and perhaps a job keep these adolescents busy. A good health history and high energy level seem to be essential for this responsible personality type.

2. Responsible parents. These children often emulate their parents. Children of responsible mothers and fathers learn their parents' style of relating with the world. Although adolescents rebel against their parents' values, some still exhibit the same underlying personality orientation. Instead of using their leadership and helping-capabilities at school, these young people may attain their power and respect from church, their social group or even another group their parents disapprove of.

Modeling isn't the only way parents influence their children's movements toward certain personality orientations. They may actively "train" their children to be responsible types. Family schedules, regular eating and sleeping times, homework supervision and required chores are all common in responsible teenagers' homes. Through these activities, parents subtly teach the basic value of responsibility.

3. Severe discipline and intense physical punishment. Severe discipline and intense physical punishment sometimes impact young people's histories and personality development. Severe punishment normally produces rebellious, self-demeaning or dependent teenagers. But when adolescents' other psychological supports are adequate, these young people can develop the traits their parents seek to instill in them.

Responsible teenagers seldom have physically abusive parents. Those situations are usually too damaging to produce the internal strength necessary to sustain this type of personality structure. But non-abusive, strong discipline can result in children's obedience to a value structure supporting responsibility.

4. Inadequate care. When parents don't provide adequate care for their children, sometimes a responsible personality develops. Most children express anger and depression through delinquency or destructive behavior, but sometimes young people find other sources of emotional support and respond by overcoming their negative feelings and experiences. When responsible personalities result from inadequate parental care, these teenagers have compensated or overcompensated for their early-life deficiencies. When this is true, unmet emotional needs plus repressed pain and anger accompany these teenagers' external presentations of strength, warmth and "having it all together." While responsible behavior in "Teenager A" may indicate a strong personality development, identical behavior in "Teenager B" can signal overcompensation. This type of personal history is a powerful example of why parents need to understand their teenagers' backgrounds.

5. Adequate nurturing. Adequate nurturing is a common discovery in responsible teenagers' backgrounds. Some degree of positive self-esteem is necessary to support the responsible social orientation. Strong parental interest and adequate nurturing are typical ingredients for developing this type of inner strength. Children learn about who they are and what attitudes to have toward themselves primarily from how their parents and significant others treat them. This is why it's vital that parents respond lovingly and positively toward their children. Essentially, they're teaching their children how to think and feel about themselves. And by the time young people reach adolescence, these attitudes are well-established and difficult to alter.

Many responsible young people have grown up in families that reinforce responsible behavior. They've been taught to feel good about themselves when their attitudes and actions follow responsible patterns.

"You certainly do a fine job of keeping your room clean."

"I appreciate your willingness to help."

"I'm impressed with your grades! You're so conscientious."

These positive comments support behavior common to responsible personality types.

6. Assuming responsibility early in life. Some young people described in this chapter began adopting a responsible orientation early in life. Life may present situations that invite responsible behavior. Young children in single-parent families may be expected to assume more responsibility. Parents working outside the home may have neither time nor energy left for normal household duties. They expect their children to assume more responsibility.

Older children may assume various responsibilities such as taking care of younger brothers and sisters or assisting with many household chores. By completing their tasks, young people receive reinforcement for being responsible, contributing family members. In this way they also identify themselves as people who help others and take active group leadership roles.

7. Pain and failure. Some responsible teenagers may have experienced pain and failure during earlier childhood. They may have felt rejected by their friends and classmates. Others may have received poor grades or were chosen last when the class divided into teams. Children who have felt put down, rejected or isolated by others often succumb to rebellious, self-demeaning or dependent personality adjustments. But responsible teenagers who experience these unfortunate childhood incidents have enough inner strength and external support to compensate for their earlier pain. They've refused to give in to adversity. Their responsible orientation expresses their efforts to prevent a recurrence of those painful experiences. They believe that through self-reliance, personal strength, active involvement and warm friendships they can live happy, fulfilling lives. Their choice of a responsible lifestyle represents an escape from pain and a commitment to positive, effective living.

8. Reinforcement. As pre-adolescent and early adolescent young people find that others depend on them, their responsible social orientation is reinforced. They learn that others not only like and respect them, but seek to be with them.

Experiencing others' dependency enhances their good feelings about themselves. It reinforces their sense of personal value and helps them believe they have something valuable to offer. As long as others' dependency isn't smothering, it can provide the basis for satisfying, meaningful relationships.

Responding to another's needs keeps responsible teenagers from thinking about their own weaknesses. When they aren't confronted by their own pain, their internal feelings of failure or questions about their personal worth, they feel more comfortable. Focusing on others' needs helps them avoid their inner tension and reinforces their good feelings about their value to others. This reinforcement also increases the probability that they'll continue to use the same type of responsible behavior.

9. Exposure to tragedy. A responsible social orientation sometimes develops during childhood or early adolescence when young people are exposed to others' pain or tragedies. Contact with people experiencing serious emotional or physical pain often draws intense compassion, sympathy and desires to help. A friend may suffer the death of a parent, brother or sister. A buddy's parents may divorce. A relative may suffer through a terminal illness. Family friends may experience a severe financial reversal. There are many other less drastic but painful experiences that friends and relatives may confront. Breaking up with a girlfriend or boyfriend, being cut from an athletic team, losing an important game, breaking an arm or leg, having surgery, losing a school election or being rejected by an important peer group—all these experiences are extremely painful for young people.

Responding to people in physical or emotional pain often brings satisfaction and fulfillment. To see another's smile or receive an appreciative hug indicates the importance of a teenager's comfort and compassion. Helping others makes young people feel important and helps them recognize their value as they extend themselves to others. These experiences help develop important parts of their self-concepts. "I'm a compassionate and sympathetic person." "I'm a generous and helping individual." Helping-acts and concern prepare these young people to develop a responsible personality orientation as they move into adolescence.

10. Self-reinforcement. Teenagers develop different personality patterns because these behavior patterns work for them. Each pattern reduces anxiety that comes from close contact with others. Each orientation gives adolescents a way to view themselves. Each provides a pattern adolescents can rely on for interacting with others. The responsible orientation is usually heavily reinforced by adults and teenagers' peers. The responsible personality orientation works well in our culture because others value the behaviors and attitudes expressed by this personality type.

Identifying factors that contribute to the responsible orientation's development helps us understand these young people. When we know where they've come from and what made them the way they are, we're better prepared to help them meet their needs. Our knowledge and support can help these young people adapt more positively to this world.

► Healthy Forms of the Responsible Personality

Some teenagers present healthy, positive functioning in their responsible adaptation. These young people have found ways to become valuable members of their family, church and school. They've adapted their personality type in ways that help them feel good about themselves. They've integrated responsibility's stronger values into their identities. Not every aspect of their social and personal functioning is positive, but the overwhelming picture is one of healthy adolescent development.

The Helper. Marvin is a 17-year-old high school junior. He's an active member of his church youth group and is popular both at school and in church. During a recent consultation session with a group of youth workers, one of Marvin's adult youth sponsors discussed him as an example of the responsible type of teenager. She reported that he is actively involved in many kids' lives. He's a good mechanic and freely gives his time and talent to repair his friends' cars. He's also excellent in math and regularly tutors others in his classes. Even when his teachers grade on a curve, he continues helping his classmates excel in their exams. He offers rides to and from school, church youth meetings, Bible study, football and basketball games and other activities. And he provides his friends interest-free loans.

In some ways Marvin reminds us of Walter, the servant and self-demeaning personality in Chapter 5. Both find meaning in helping others. The primary difference is in each boy's attitude toward himself. Walter believes the only thing he has to offer is his servitude. He has little belief in himself; and no matter how much he does for others, his self-esteem remains low and unsatisfactory. Marvin also helps his friends. Yet, there's a difference in the quality and attitude of Marvin's helping. Marvin enjoys everything he does. He's eager to help in almost any way he can. There's no hint of a self-demeaning attitude when he does something for others; in fact, he enjoys helping so much that he makes others around him feel better too.

Marvin has been involved in his church youth group only since the summer before his sophomore year. Some of his friends who were already members invited him to join them on a 1,000-mile bike-hike. During this experience he made a personal commitment to Christ and developed a close relationship with the youth minister. After the trip, Marvin began attending Sunday school and youth meetings. He quickly became a popular, valued group member.

Marvin grew up in a traditional family environment. His father worked on the assembly line in an automobile-manufacturing plant. He worked shifts, so his schedule changed every six months. His mother stayed home, but contributed to the family finances by taking in laundry, doing ironing and providing mending and seamstress services.

Marvin was the second of four children. Each child had regular chores and was expected to contribute to the family in whatever extra ways were needed. The values of working together, pooling their resources for the common good and helping one another were taught by example, direction and family structure. Marvin learned his lessons well. He embraced these values as important rules to live by. He also formed much of his interpersonal orientation and personality development around these integral principles evident in his family.

To Marvin, a good, worthwhile person means being helpful and considerate of others. It means being responsible and following the rules. It means expressing generosity and genuine concern. He felt good about himself when he acted according to these ideals. Guilt pangs stabbed him the few times he decided to place his interests above family's and friends'. Marvin's helping attitude and efforts won reinforcement from those around him; his social pattern became fixed. His style of interacting with others and adjusting to the world became central to the way he saw himself. He developed an adaptive, healthy form of the responsible personality type.

The Reliable. Wayne is a high school senior who lives with his mother and younger brother in a moderate-sized city. His mother is a clinical social worker in private practice at a psychotherapy center. Wayne's father is an attorney who had problems with compulsive gambling and women. When Wayne's parents were together, their combined income was over $100,000 per year. Wayne's father squandered thousands of dollars each year on gambling, but they avoided financial ruin because Wayne's mother was a good money manager. Finally, after struggling through three of her husband's affairs, Wayne's mother filed for divorce. Following a 16-month settlement dispute, the court determined that she and the two boys could stay in the family home until the younger son graduated from high school. Wayne was 7 years old when his parents' divorce was final.

After listening to many parental arguments and discussions about the dangers of gambling, Wayne is well aware of the risks of uncontrolled impulses. Even though he didn't understand the terms, from early childhood he learned firsthand how compulsive behavior patterns and poor impulse control can destroy family life and personal happiness. From his mother he also learned the value of responsibility, consistency and reliability—strong traits that helped her family survive those difficult times. He observed her as she worked extremely hard, even increasing her caseload, to meet her family's increased financial demands.

As a young child, Wayne began to grasp the seriousness of their financial plight and learned to value his mother's wise and consistent managing of their family finances. He wanted to emulate her responsible attitude. He began looking for opportunities to help. During childhood and early adolescence, he felt guilty when he shirked responsibilities, did a sloppy job or was lazy. He knew those actions let his mother down. He remembered how his father had repeatedly fallen short of her expectations, and he didn't want to be like his dad. He didn't want his mother to be angry with him like she'd been angry with his father. Unconsciously, Wayne feared that she'd leave him also if he disappointed her too frequently. He resolved to do all he could to please his mother; he had to be a good person.

Wayne consistently completed his chores at home. He was equally reliable in being on time and turning in his completed schoolwork. His teachers, and his mother learned to depend on him. His word was totally trustworthy; he did what he said he'd do. He wasn't as energetic or efficient as Marvin, the helper, earlier in this chapter, but he was a dependable, trustworthy and totally reliable 17-year-old.

The Overachiever. Sharon is one of the most outstanding members of her graduating class. She has been extremely active all four years of high school. Although her IQ is just slightly above average, she produces a straight-"A" average on almost every report card. She's active in school student government and every year has been elected to positions such as student council representative, class vice president, class president and student-body president. Sharon's classmates recognize her as a great organizer and director of campus events and group projects.

She also participates in competitive team sports. She plays forward on the girls basketball team, and enjoys tennis. Her skillful serve and ability to rush the net have earned her first singles player's position on the girls tennis team. Volleyball and swimming round out her athletic activities.

Sharon's energetic lifestyle extends to her church youth group. Although her primary focus is school, she's also involved in church leadership. She has taken piano lessons since second grade and plays for her Sunday-morning high school class. She's on the social committee and is one of two student representatives from the youth group to the church board. Sharon has also taken training in one-to-one discipling of new members.

Where does Sharon get all her energy? Why does she choose to be so actively involved? A look at her family gives some clues. She's the elder of two children. Her 13-year-old brother is almost as busy as she is. Their father is a corporate executive who has worked 10 to 16 hours a day, six days a week until the past two years. As an executive vice president, he's finally delegated many of his responsibilities. He now works only 10- to 12-hour days, but has his weekends free. Sharon's mom doesn't work outside the home, but both parents are heavily involved socially, at church and in both their children's schools. Her mother is also active in their precinct's political activities.

Sharon has inherited a high metabolism level that contributes to her extreme activity. She's learned from her parents to look for and take advantage of new or exciting opportunities. Her parents have stressed the value of setting goals and achieving them. Her whole family seeks external success symbols as indicators of their personal okayness. Everyone in Sharon's family values having the right friends, being seen with the right people, wearing the "in" styles, driving the right cars and participating in the right activities. Though Sharon enjoys her activities, she seems driven by a fear of missing out on something. Her need for personal affirmation makes it painful for her to let go or say no to any additional worthwhile activity.

► Unhealthy Forms of the Responsible Personality

Teenagers who've developed an unhealthy form of the responsible social orientation often go unnoticed by their parents. On the surface their behavior may look not only normal but typical and responsible. Their problem's core is their excessive need to be normal and acceptable. Their behavior expresses an uncontrollable need to be liked and respected.

These young people restrict their activities to those they perceive as acceptable to others. They do everything to please others and lose contact with their own expectations and desires. They are no longer capable of establishing their own value system. Here are some examples that might help you identify and help your unhealthy responsible adolescents.

The Little Adult. Fifteen-year-old Oliver and his parents met his counselor at their church while the man was presenting a meeting series on parent-teen relationships. At the close of each of the six sessions, Oliver sought out the therapist and asked him several thoughtful questions about adolescence, families and communication. His parents joined their son's discussions with the counselor at the end of the last two sessions. A few weeks after the series ended, Oliver's father called to initiate counseling for his son.

Oliver was well-liked by his teachers, youth minister and other adults who worked with him. He was also popular with his peers. He was serious and contemplative, and at first appearance seemed extremely mature. Even with limited contact, however, his counselor discovered that Oliver's attempt to appear grown-up was actually a "pseudo maturity." He could present a facade or behavior that looked mature, but this was only a performance. Oliver had no identity development to give his behavior any real substance. All his actions gave an impression of maturity without exhibiting maturity itself. Oliver had unconsciously designed his facade to present the trait he lacked.

Oliver lacked teenagers' normal youthful spontaneity and exuberance. He seldom joined others as they joked, teased and played around. He could handle group activities only if they were organized and structured, and then he demanded that rules be impeccably followed. He felt indignant when his sense of justice was violated, but seldom released his anger where others could see it. Oliver tightly controlled all his emotions. He feared his anger might get out of control. He also feared others might reject him if they saw how he really was on the inside.

People seldom saw Oliver show any emotional expression. He always responded logically and rationally. He prided himself on his ability to think clearly. He felt superior because of his apparent exemption from strong, potentially disruptive attacks of extreme emotion so common among early and mid-adolescents.

Oliver's therapist quickly saw that he was quite immature in his social development. Oliver represented a combination of the helper and reliable forms of the responsible personality type, but to an extreme. He felt free to interact with his peers only in safe, proper, almost formal ways. Otherwise, he was withdrawn and passive around other teenagers. He was especially immature in his relationships with girls. He could relate to them only in a caretaking or parenting role. According to Oliver's youth minister, girls respected and liked him, although they thought he was a little odd.

Several individual therapy sessions with Oliver plus two family counseling sessions provided family history and interpersonal dynamics that helped his therapist understand why Oliver developed his personality structure. Oliver's father chose an Army career, and both his parents had strong, conservative religious commitments. Their home life and family expectations reflected the tight structure common to both disciplines. Oliver's parents fully expected him to meet their expectations and conform to their values, attitudes and perceptions.

His family was very loving. With no brothers or sisters, Oliver didn't have to share his parents' ample affection and positive attention. They reinforced his conformity and good behavior with more attention and affection, but responded to his few episodes of misbehavior with temporary withdrawal of support, strong verbal reprimands and an occasional spanking.

The combined forces of Oliver's home environment strongly impacted his personality development. The tight structuring of the military and religious orientations, heavy reinforcement of conformity, threat of withdrawn affection and attention and the underlying assurance of his parents' love were key elements in Oliver's personality formation.

His family's frequent relocations necessitated by his father's military career also affected Oliver's social development. He was adept at forming new relationships, but had virtually no experience developing long-term friendships. Therefore, his friendships and relationships were based on what he perceived others wanted, needed or expected rather than expressing the person Oliver had developed into.

The Neurotic. Vanessa was a 17-year-old high school senior when she entered professional counseling. Her youth minister had counseled her for many hours, as had two female volunteer youth leaders in her church. Finally, with the youth minister's encouragement, Vanessa's parents took her to the Christian therapist he recommended.

Several things about Vanessa struck her counselor as she entered her first counseling session. Vanessa's perfectionism was immediately apparent. Her skirt and blazer were freshly pressed and coordinated, her hair and nails were perfectly groomed and her makeup was flawless. Her tense body reflected the worry and apprehension she carried with her every day. Stress had etched lines of concern in her forehead and tightened every muscle in her body. She was extremely thin and taut. She was also excessively eager to please. She looked to her counselor for indications of what he wanted her to do. She desperately needed to know the rules for behavior. With no cues to guide her, she wasn't sure what was appropriate in this new environment. These initial impressions were merely surface indications of Vanessa's deep, enduring personality traits.

Vanessa was the youngest of four children. Her parents, brothers and sister had been unusually eager to meet her needs and wants. While very young, she'd learned how to maneuver each family member into serving her. This ability to manipulate others had produced a strong self-centered orientation that worked throughout her elementary school years at school and church, in addition to her home.

As Vanessa moved into middle school, however, things began to change. No longer were her friends willing to treat her like a queen. They began rejecting her demands for attention and service. By November of her sixth-grade year, she was isolated and rejected by her previously close school friends. And she experienced the same rejection in her church youth group.

Throughout the next few years, Vanessa floundered socially. She was confused, frustrated, lonely and depressed much of the time. During her sophomore year she finally began to change. Her biology teacher, Mrs. Bryson, noticed her struggling and asked Vanessa to help her with some special projects. While they worked together in the lab, they talked.

Mrs. Bryson listened carefully and gained Vanessa's trust. After a time this gentle teacher helped Vanessa see how her self-centeredness had turned others away. Vanessa gradually recognized she was largely responsible for her friends' negative reactions. She realized she'd have to change the way she treated others if she wanted them to accept her.

Vanessa consciously decided she would pattern her life and relationships after her parents'. Her parents had been church leaders as long as she could remember. Her father was a respected community businessman, and her mother volunteered in several charitable clubs and committees. Both were known, liked and well-respected in their community. They seemed to have their lives well-organized and under control. Everything about them appeared stable.

As Vanessa recovered from her pain of rejection and her exclusion from meaningful relationships, she adopted a new social orientation. She decided she wanted to always be appropriate and do what was expected. She didn't want to disappoint anyone. She decided she'd always be kind, giving and helpful to others.

Vanessa became intolerant of any weaknesses she perceived in herself. Personal weakness and inadequacy represented major threats to her hopes for peer acceptance. She became extreme in her external presentation, believing her worth came from the way others saw her. Her excessive concern about her performance caused her to lose sight of her inner being. She lost contact with her inner feelings and motivations. She became excessively restricted, lacked creativity and began demanding perfection from herself in everything.

Though she usually earned straight "A's," Vanessa dreaded every test. She was sure she wouldn't pass. Following most of her exams and assignments, she was certain she had failed. She was always surprised at each "A."

Friendships also made Vanessa anxious and fearful. She was extremely nervous about what others thought of her. She felt she had to comply perfectly with all rules and expectations to be socially acceptable to her friends. In relationships she could tolerate herself only as a helper or giver and would never allow herself to receive from others.

Vanessa's anxiety level had become destructive to her physical and emotional well-being. She experienced insomnia, loss of appetite, weight loss, an inability to concentrate, lack of interest in her daily activities and other depression symptoms. She seemed agitated and nervous, talked compulsively and couldn't stop pacing and fidgeting. Her symptoms clearly resulted from her unhealthy intensity in being a responsible young person. Vanessa had become neurotic in her adolescent personality development; she was obsessed by her need to be responsible.

► Effects of Responsible Behavior on Others

The responsible personality type represents one of our society's most ideal and desirable lifestyles. Our society and the Christian community generally prize the values supporting this social orientation. Strength, self-reliance, self-control, reason, logic, helping others, obeying rules, respecting traditions and sympathetic concern for others are fundamental to this interpersonal orientation.

Because the underlying values of the responsible personality type are socially desirable, people typically respond positively to this type of teenager. Many young people like to form a dependent relationship with a responsible adolescent; they see their strength and leadership qualities and find security relying on them. This dependency also fulfills the responsible teenager's need by reinforcing his or her fantasies of personal strength, social power and helpfulness.

Cooperation is another common reaction others have to a responsible teenager. When young people can give their allegiance to a responsible-oriented adolescent without sacrificing their personal dignity or self-respect, they find it much easier to cooperate. With the responsible personality type, others don't fear losing their personal value.

A responsible teenager also receives respect, acclaim and popularity from adults and peers. This young person epitomizes the behavior and interaction styles valued by most of our society. Adults are pleasantly surprised when they interact with one of these teenagers. They're impressed with these young people's apparent maturity and competence. A responsible young person is often valued more highly by peers than by his or her personal evaluation. Peers assume the responsible teenager is brighter, functions at a higher level, and operates in a more competent social manner than they do. Other teenagers like a responsible adolescent, consider him or her popular and seek that valuable friendship. The compassionate strength of the responsible adolescent draws respect and admiration from everyone he or she associates with.

Some teenagers, particularly competitive, aggressive and rebellious ones, often react with frustration and anger to a responsible teenager because they don't feel equal. Some of these reactions come from the personality struggles and defenses inside the other teenagers; some, however, are responses to the power operations that the responsible teenager uses. When young people are excessive in their responsible behavior, they may receive negative reactions. When their actions become so extreme that they seem out of touch with reality, others may become bored or disinterested and are likely to withdraw.

► Guidelines for Parenting Responsible Adolescents

Parents are usually proud of their responsible adolescents. These young people often relate easily to most adults and are usually popular with their peers. Responsible-oriented young people present few behavioral problems; however, you can benefit from suggestions on how to meet your adolescents' special needs. After reviewing this chapter, the following suggestions offer additional help as you parent your responsible teenagers.

1. Try to understand how your teenagers think and feel by carefully observing their behavior. Little children almost always express their feelings and attitudes through their actions. Adults usually discuss their opinions and emotions. Adolescents do some of both but most likely express their inner thoughts and feelings through behavior. They may express their happiness, affection, anger or uncertainty. When expressions of their internal feelings overcome their intended actions, we say these young people have a behavioral problem.

If you haven't already, now is a great time to observe your teenagers' behaviors. Use dialogue and discussion to check how accurately you understand what your teenagers are doing and why. Through verbal interaction you can provide opportunities for your young people to put their feelings into words.

"Each of us finds ways of relating to others that help us feel good about ourselves. I've noticed you seem to enjoy helping your friends with their math homework. How do you feel when they call you for help?"

"Son, I think it's great you're so busy at school and church. It's neat to be popular and active. But are you finding any time to slow down and think? Sometimes continuous activity protects us from getting to know ourselves better. What do you think?"

Discuss your observations of your teenagers' actions and prompt them to question their feelings of responsibility. Help your young people determine whether what they're doing is for themselves or because others expect it.

2. Reinforce your responsible teenagers' strengths. Teenagers, especially responsible-oriented young people, want to please their parents. They respond well to appreciation and compliments. The more you notice, accept and appreciate them, the more highly motivated they'll be to make positive changes. Nothing succeeds like success. Tell your young people that you see and value their personal strengths.

"Sue, I can't tell you how proud I am of how well you've handled being a student-body officer this year. It's put a lot of pressure on you, but you've managed extremely well! You've certainly developed a lot of personal strength during this experience."

"Mark, it must've been tough not to give in to the temptation to use drugs last night at the party. Sounds like almost everyone was involved. You showed a lot of character by saying no, and I'm proud of you."

In addition to discussing your appreciation for their strengths and accomplishments, emphasize your confidence in their abilities by letting your teenagers take family leadership roles. Encourage them to plan vacations, set up household-chore schedules and plan dinner menus. Tell your responsible young people that you value their abilities and strengths.

3. Encourage your responsible adolescents in their tendencies toward compassion and caring for others. Responsible teenagers feel good about themselves when they show love and kindness to others. They feel comfortable when they give to others, even though they need to learn to receive. Tell your teenagers how much you appreciate and value their compassion, care and help for others. Reward their kind gestures and congratulate their willingness to extend themselves to their friends.

Do something special for your teenagers when they're kind to an unpopular child at school or church. Write them appreciative notes to tell them you're aware of their special qualities. Take them out to dinner, or prepare their favorite meal at home.

Encourage your responsible teenagers to take leadership in a family helping project. Maybe they could be in charge of collecting items for the family's special package to send to missionaries. Perhaps they might research what it takes to support a needy child through an organized missions project or nearby orphanage; then they could help the family implement this project. Ask your teenagers to manage the collection of canned food or toys for needy families in your church, community or neighborhood. Your responsible teenagers benefit greatly from your encouragement as they lead your family in these caring projects.

4. Help your young people relax their self-control. While many parents are actively praying for their adolescents to learn self-control, many responsible-oriented teenagers hold themselves under too rigid controls. The extremity of their self-control expresses an underlying distrust in themselves. They're afraid that relaxing control of their feelings and actions will get them into trouble. Often they experience strong anxiety about their aggressive and sexual impulses, leading them to repress, deny and "overcontrol" their behavior. As a parent, you're in a key position to encourage them to relax their critical self-observation and tight self-controls.

Brenda presents a good example of an adolescent who

takes self-control to an extreme. Brenda strictly adheres to a modest but well-balanced diet of fish, chicken, vegetables and fruit. In addition, she's designed an extremely tight schedule for herself. Each morning she spends a half-hour reading her Bible and praying. Immediately after school she completes her homework. She practices her oboe 45 minutes every evening, except on Thursday when she has her lesson. Every Saturday morning she cleans and straightens her room, does her laundry and completes her ironing before she does anything with her friends.

Brenda's parents appreciate their daughter's self-control, but they also recognize her unwillingness to make any exceptions to her routine. They've talked with her about their concerns and encouraged her to allow some flexibility in her schedule. She's gradually gained confidence in her ability to continue being responsible while loosening her self-control.

You can provide the same kind of guidance to your responsible teenagers. Help them question their rigid behaviors. Offer your acceptance and encouragement for a more flexible schedule. Your support helps these compulsive young people accept themselves without their extreme forms of self-control.

5. Help your teenagers relax their demands for perfection. Many responsible adolescents become excessive perfectionists in their personal demands of themselves. They feel highly threatened by any signs of their own imperfections, weaknesses or inadequacies. Their perfectionism may signal extreme insecurity and fear beneath their facade of competence and adequacy. Your parenting task is to help them become more comfortable and secure with themselves by assuring them that you unconditionally love and accept them. As they experience your care and acceptance, even when they make serious mistakes, they begin to learn that their inherent value doesn't come from their perfection.

When Mark began to demand straight "A's" of himself and berated himself for an occasional "B," his parents decided not to differentiate between the two grades. They congratulated him the same way for both "A's" and "B's." They told him they were proud of his ability to do well in school, but reassured him that perfect grades were not why they loved him.

Sheila's parents began to notice her drive for perfection when she insisted on always being the "perfect daughter." She became extremely rule-conscious. She chose only the right friends, participated in only acceptable activities, took only college-prep classes and wore only those clothes appropriate for her figure type. She also made sure her behavior was always mature.

Sheila's parents resisted her additional attempts to mold them into a perfect pattern. Although they sometimes embarrassed Sheila, they chose to not always dress in the most appropriate style. They openly laughed at their mistakes and tried to help Sheila relax and not take herself so seriously. In actions and words, her parents communicated that her perfection wasn't essential for their pride in her as their lovable, wonderful daughter.

Both Mark's and Sheila's parents acted to reduce their children's perfectionism. They displayed acceptable standards with their behaviors and continued maintaining control of their lives according to their own rules. Both sets of parents modeled acceptable behaviors without the perfection that their adolescents insisted on.

6. Encourage your young people to respond spontaneously. As a result of excessive self-control and personal demands for perfection, these teenagers can't express their feelings and thoughts spontaneously. They become pensive, deliberate, intense young people who need moments of spontaneous release and play. These adolescents tend to internalize and then repress their negative emotions. They sometimes carry tremendous burdens of concern and worry.

Part of your parenting task is to help your responsible teenagers feel self-confident and secure enough to enjoy spontaneity. Consider these ways to help your young people accomplish this goal:

• Remind yourself of the powerful impact of effective modeling, and exhibit spontaneity in your life.

• Tell a joke the moment you think of it, even if the timing isn't appropriate.

• Laugh out loud sometime when it's socially correct to

be subdued.

- Decide to fly a kite, go roller-skating or play ball with your young person instead of mowing the lawn, even when the grass is threatening to swallow the flower bed.
- Illustrate in your life what you want your young people to express in their lives.
- Risk being lighthearted and tease them gently and lovingly. "You know, David, I bet going to the game today wouldn't make you flunk out of school." "Wait a minute, Barbara. What's the worst thing that could happen if you did lose control and laugh during prayer time?"

Help your teenagers see that periodic spontaneity won't bring catastrophic results.

7. Allow and, if necessary, even encourage your adolescents to rebel in acceptable ways. Parents of competitive, aggressive and rebellious teenagers have difficulty understanding why parents would ever encourage their adolescents to rebel. These parents expend tremendous energy and experience intense heartache when they try to control their excessively rebellious teenagers. But sometimes responsible young people are too insecure to actively rebel against anyone or anything. Rebelling against a parent or another authority figure feels too risky. The fear of being rejected and condemned is too great.

Your parenting task is to help these young people develop the courage to risk enough appropriate rebellious behavior to establish their own sense of identity. Resist telling your teenagers what you think about a situation until they've fully expressed their own thoughts and feelings. Don't make it easy for them to conform to your perceptions. Prod them to explore and discover their own feelings and attitudes.

"Josh, I'm interested in what you have to say about this newspaper headline. You usually have interesting ideas about this sort of thing."

"Sure, I'll tell you what I think. But first I want to hear what you think about it."

When your responsible adolescents finally express some signs of rebellion, reassure them it's okay to be different from you. Tell them you're eager to see how they'll develop into their own adult personalities. Bring to their attention some of their perceptions and attitudes that are different from yours. Discuss these differences so they understand that being different doesn't threaten their sense of belonging and the parental relationship that's so important to your teenagers.

8. Accept your teenagers' weaknesses. Responsible teenagers typically feel threatened by their weaknesses and inadequacies. They fear that the personal flaws they perceive in themselves will cause others to reject them. Their need for personal perfection prevents them from accepting areas of incompetence in themselves. This inability to accept their inadequacies seriously impedes their psychological and social development during adolescence.

You can dramatically influence your young people to accept themselves more fully. Through a parental attitude of acceptance, teenagers learn that self-rejection is unnecessary and undesirable. These young people can piggyback on your accepting attitude while they develop their own self-acceptance.

You can help your responsible teenagers accept their weaknesses. Remember to encourage and accept your young people when they fail. They may be cut from an athletic squad, lose a class election, receive a failing grade, be fired from a job or experience a good friend's rejection. These adolescents usually blame themselves for all the negative things that happen to them. Your love and emotional support at these sensitive times can soften your teenagers' tendencies to punish themselves.

Your teenagers sometimes disappoint you and don't live up to your expectations. Tell them how you feel, what you expect and what they can do to improve and correct the situation. Focus on your teenagers' behaviors, not their character. You need to do this in a way that provides opportunities for reconciliation and new beginnings. "I want you to change your behavior" is a much better approach than, "You're acting stupidly." Always tell your adolescents that it's your feeling about their behavior you're having trouble accepting. Rejection limited only to their behaviors continues to provide opportunities for reconciliation, new beginnings and growth for both you and your adolescents.

9. Encourage your teenagers to risk depending on someone else and still feel good about it. Responsible young people usually feel guilty about their dependency needs. They feel vulnerable and insecure when they have to depend on someone else. They unconsciously say, "I'm secure only when I'm strong, helping and independent." Dependency feels dangerous to these young people. Reassure your teenagers that adolescence is a development period when it's normal to fluctuate between independence and dependence. These young people need to know they have personal value when they're dependent and independent.

You can perform a valuable function when you help your teenagers accept their dependency needs. Provide opportunities at home for periodic discussions of each family member's strengths. Focus on the benefits the whole family gains from each member. Celebrate each person's special gifts and thank each one for his or her contribution. Discuss how your family represents the body of Christ with each member fulfilling his or her function. Stress your need for one another and emphasize the value of interdependence.

10. Help your teenagers accept their emotions and thoughts.
Responsible young people need to learn that their emotions are as much a part of normal, healthy living as their thoughts. These adolescents distrust their emotions and believe they must keep them under tight control. They feel insecure and vulnerable when they experience and express strong feelings. Fears and concerns multiply because of the heightened intensity and wider extremes of emotions prevalent during adolescence. When dealing with these strong emotional impulses, teenagers are threatened by their inability to maintain particular images. Responsible teenagers see any loss of control of their emotions as unacceptable.

You can help and reassure your young people. Constructively express your emotions in front of your teenagers. Allow yourself to cry, laugh, raise your voice in anger, extend sympathetic compassion and admit anxiety and fear. Let your teenagers see that strong emotions aren't always destructive. The way you handle your feelings can encourage your young people through your example's impact.

Be open and accept your teenagers when they express

their emotions. Don't expect perfect or appropriate behaviors. Let them make mistakes without strong disciplinary reactions. Remember these young people are just learning to accomplish a difficult task that many adults never master. They'll probably shout too loud, feel sorry for themselves too long and become infatuated with partners who don't meet your expectations. Remember to respond to them with patience and understanding. Trust them to learn and mature through their experiences. Remain open and available when they need to discuss their intense feelings and when they ask for your help or opinion.

11. Allow and encourage your young people to express some aggressiveness. Responsible-oriented teenagers have difficulty risking any confrontation through aggressive expressions, even in moderation. They hesitate because they fear rejection. They also fear being seen as uncaring and selfish. They willingly deny all their aggressive impulses to protect themselves from losing self-respect or experiencing others' condemnation. These adolescents need help to integrate their aggressive traits with the rest of their personality.

You can play an important role in giving these teenagers the help they need. Discuss openly the wide variety of aggressive models that movies and television present to us. Discuss how different types and intensities of aggression work in various settings. Point out the necessity of the more extreme types of aggression in hostile environments such as war and violent crime. Discuss the appropriateness of milder forms of aggression such as honesty and direct expressions of thoughts and feelings. Help your young people see that these milder forms of aggression contain no desire to hurt others, but contribute to most social interactions, especially in the family. During these discussions be sure to ask what your teenagers think about these forms of aggression. Don't just lecture!

Let your young people make judgment errors. Let them make mistakes without losing their dignity. First, listen to what they have to say. Discuss what happened. Then, sparingly and briefly, tell them your observations. Avoid making judgments. Assure them there's always a next time to try again.

Encourage them to practice their aggression at home. Don't worry about these young people making the household a battleground. Remember, they're usually reticent to express even mild aggression, so let them practice their confrontive skills on you. It's better for them to make mistakes in their secure home environment so they can function confidently in other relationships.

12. Help increase your teenagers' self-awareness. The first step toward growth is gaining awareness. Confession can't take place without consciousness of what one is confessing. Your teenagers can't change their attitudes, perceptions, thoughts, feelings or behavior without first becoming aware of who they are and how they wish to be. The family should provide the most secure environment for gaining this awareness. Once teenagers feel safe and accepted as they are, subsequent movements toward change can occur.

You can facilitate your young people's increasing self-awareness. Encourage your teenagers to talk about themselves. Avoid the parental tendency to do most of the talking. This is particularly important when your young people are quiet and withdrawn. Let them know you're genuinely interested in what they have to say. Don't hound and probe; rather, invite them to tell you their thoughts and feelings.

Then wait patiently as they slowly move into a position in which they feel comfortable opening up to you. Remember, talking, especially about anything negative, is difficult for responsible teenagers because they often feel they're risking their dignity. Seek to accept and refuse to judge what they reveal. The amount of openness you experience from them depends on how well you receive what they choose to share.

Be more open about yourself. This encourages openness in your teenagers. As your adolescents begin to know you as a real person with faults and weaknesses, you become less threatening to them. One early-adolescent client recently told his therapist: "Since my dad started letting me see some of his faults, it's easier for me to let him see some of mine. I always thought he was almost perfect. Now I'm glad he's not. If he has problems, then maybe he won't be so critical of me!"

13. Encourage your teenagers to establish their own standards of acceptable behavior rather than accept their peers'. Responsible young people are especially conscious of current guidelines for appropriate behavior. As they mature through adolescence, they need to develop inner strengths to determine what's right and wrong for them.

Effective parenting includes helping your teenagers become increasingly responsible for their choices. During regular conversations with your adolescents, show an interest in knowing what they think.

"I'm curious as to what you think about that."

"You know how your teacher voted. Now how would you have voted if you were 18?"

"I think you know how we view having sex before marriage. But what's even more important is what you think about it."

Sometimes it's important for you to support your teenagers' strength to stand against their peers. Affirm them when they decide to live by their own conscience rather than their peers'. Encourage them to discuss their temptations to conform. Invite them to discuss and recognize their fears of rejection. Remind them of your support and assure them of God's strengthening presence as they struggle with these difficult decisions.

We've examined the responsible adolescent personality in some depth. We've surveyed ways of parenting these young people. As you identify responsible teenagers in your family, review this chapter to prepare yourself to meet their needs. Remember to accept and build on their strengths. But prepare yourself to be supportive and trustworthy to help these young people struggle with their growth and maturity, qualities essential to their complete personality development.

Closing Comments

Now that you have familiarized yourself with these eight styles of social interaction, you have a deeper understanding of your teenager's personality. You know that your young person's interpersonal behavior gives valuable insight into the needs and motives that give rise to that behavior. You have also discovered that each of your child's personality traits has both positive and negative expressions. You know to look at the level of intensity and the degree of appropriateness of the behavior to determine the healthiness of your teenager's reactions.

Remember, your adolescent is developing his or her identity. Teenagers' interpersonal orientations are likely to go through several changes. Along with their youth comes flexibility. Avoid rigidly categorizing your teenager into one of the eight interpersonal styles, assuming that no significant personal changes will ever occur. Doing this causes parents to miss seeing subtle changes and growth in their children.

Look for the good in your teenager's behavior. Reinforce the positive aspects of his or her social orientation. Develop your understanding of the meaning which underlies the unhealthy behavior. Don't just react to the behavior. Rather, try to respond effectively to meet the needs expressed through your teenager's actions.

Our task . . . our opportunity . . . as parents is to nurture and encourage our children to develop into the people God created them to be. We aren't the final determiners of exactly who our young people will become. But we do play a major role in impacting the course of their development. Equipping ourselves with knowledge and insight is one of our responsibilities as we seek to fulfill our task as parents. It is to this end that *What Makes* Your *Teenager Tick* has been written.